J. WRICE SR. PRESENTS:

KARESSA' VAULT

IN

ONE WAY OUT

THE LONE MARAUDER SERIES ONE

By Willie J. Wrice Sr.

TABLE OF CONTENTS

Chapter 1

MY RESUME

Allow me to introduce myself, my name is Karessa' Vault. My occupation, professional criminal, if I can make money from it, I'm in. The reason why I do what I do, it's easy and I'm good at it. Since the age of ten I've always wanted to be in this profession, well, if I can call it a profession.

I ran the streets with my friends and joined a gang and from there, is how I learned to steal cars, clothes, money, anything that wasn't nailed down to the floor. I never sold drugs, even though I could have made a lot of cash doing so, it wasn't a thrill in it for me. Me being a criminal isn't just about the money, it's the rush I get when my adrenaline is pumping, knowing I'm taking penitentiary chances. You got to have skills, knowledge and the art of being a thief.

Being on the street when I was younger, prepared me for this life. Most kids I know wanted to be athletes, rappers and singers, no doctors, no lawyers or anything in that area. The reason I could understand is that's all they see around them, if not that gangs and people selling drugs. What made me do what I did wasn't because I wanted to shoot or fight other gangs and be the ultimate thug of thugs. I had a mature mind at an early age, so my motivation was money. I love it, I wanted it quick, fast and in a hurry but let me take you back a moment, I lied I did sell drugs one time.

That was the only time I got caught doing something illegal. It's my first offense, but what I got arrested with and where I was selling it at had me do five months in a juvenile detention facility. Since then, the one thing I learned is not to be known to the police. And I didn't, so stealing became my thing. When I was seventeen I broke into this clothing store, well I didn't break into it I've enter it and found a spot to hide in until closing time. Staking it out for about a week before I made my move, it wasn't a huge store but a fair size one, a lot of cash is being made inside there. So on a Saturday evening is when I planted myself inside the store. I chose Saturday evening because that's when they had the most traffic, so it was easy to blend in and hide out without being noticed.

When it got close to closing time the only person left inside the store is the manager. All the employees are gone, he went into his office to count the money and do inventory. With him engulfed in his business, I came up from behind him and put my gun against his head. Acting on pure fear he begged for his life but I didn't care, I just wanted all of the cash he had in the safe and on the table. Everybody is capable of killing, but I am not a killer unless I had no choice. In this situation I had a choice I supply this equal measure to all situations I've put myself in. Once the safe was opened, I made the manager get down on his knees and close his eyes.

I told him "Good night", then struck him across the head with my weapon and knocked him out. After he'd collapse to the floor I took my time and gather all the money, took a couple of bags of clothes, slid out the back door. Sold most of the clothes, kept some for myself and counted my take. It's a little over $7500, being seventeen and growing up in a low income environment I came out like a bandit. That is the most money I've ever seen in my life at that age, all at once at one time.

At this very time is when the thirst for being a professional criminal enlighten me, this robbery boosted my ego especially since I got away with it. Even though I had friends, all the jobs I did were solo. A trust issue I guess, I didn't have to worry about anybody snitching on me if they get caught. Plus it's easier to move around by myself and all the loot that I achieve to get is all mines. Everybody I hung around with at this particular time in my life knew what I were doing, just didn't know how I kept pulling it off.

CHAPTER 2

WHO IS IT?

At the age of twenty-one, I decided to join the armed services. Not to fight for my country but to learn more tactics that could help me be more sophisticated skill wise. Doing so, I met a few soldiers who knew more than just about being all that they could be (no pun intended). They trained me in making fake identification cards, forging checks, hacking into a computer and many other useful crafts that I can implement into my line of work.

One weekend one of my soldier buddies invited me to go with her. We went to visit her cousin at the college that she attended. Doing our time there, her cousin told us about a check scam that she's been working on. She can get her hands on some bank checking books from some of the rich college kids on the campus. She has a plan that's already in play but what she needs is some fake ID's to cash the checks.

She asked my friend could she talk to our other friend at the base, the one who taught me about doing this for them. I immediately chime in and said "I can do it." Looking surprised "You can, ok, they got to be perfect though, it must look real." "No problem, it will look so real you might mistake it for your official ID." After we laugh about what I had said she gave me a large yellow envelope with all the information I needed to complete the task. She wanted me to mail it to her P.O. Box address, so I did what I was instructed. For my first time making them I must say they came out excellent. Her cousin paid me $600, when all I asked for was $350. From that she commenced to bring me some business. We formed an alliance, now I'm doing passports, then from there I learned how to make fake documents, birth certificates, bills, insurance papers, whatever a person needed to help out their situation.

Samara, who is the name of my friend's cousin, became my partner somewhat, constantly bringing me customers. But after my fourth year in the services I departed, my mind fixed not fluctuating on nothing but getting paid in a major way. Leaving the services twenty-thousand was almost made by me doing my illegal schemes. Far as Samara, we kept in contact for a while, I did a few more jobs for her then eventually, our relationship faded.

To save currency, I moved in a small crappy apartment. Nothing extravagant the neighborhood is a little dilapidated but it's a perfect place for what I need to do. After I got my new place together I went right back to business. But some time down the line the velocity of my business started to slow down. It must be another way to earn more revenue, going into my savings is not an option.

Day dreaming out of the window one day my phone rang. When I picked it up I didn't recognize the number but I answered it anyway. "Hello." the person on the other end on the phone says "Hey you, what took you so long to answer your phone?" "Samara, is that you?" "Yes ma' it's me, how have you been?" "I've been ok, just handling business as usual." "Business huh, ok, you busy right now?" "No, just looking out the window contemplating on my next move, things been slow." "Oh really, what if I can help you speed things up again." Pausing for a minute "You must got some new clients?" "I do, but in a different game, we need to sit down and talk." "We can do that, how about tomorrow, we can do brunch." "Tomorrow is fine Karessa' but let's do lunch, I have a dentist appointment in the morning but one o'clock works for me." "That's cool, how about that spot Jake's eatery, they have excellent food there." "I know where that's at, that will work, see you there."

Wondering what Samara has up her sleeve, suspicion came to mind. Not that she will be on setting me up or anything just what is she into now. And why did she contact me about it. Trying not to wreck my brain over it, I went to catch a matinee since I didn't have anything else to do. The next morning I woke up to police sirens screeching pass my apartment building.

Walking to the kitchen to fix me a cup of coffee I get a knock at my door. When I looked through the peep hole it's a police officer. So I opened the door, wiping my eyes "May I help you officer?" "Good morning pretty lady, it was a shooting around the corner from here, so I'm trying to see if you heard or seen anything?" Trying to catch my yarn "No officer, I was dead to the world actually it was your sirens that woke me up."

Smiling "I'm sorry we woke you out of your beauty sleep, maybe I can give you my number and I could take you out to make up for the disturbance." Soft laughter "Well maybe, I can't believe you are hitting on me, when I look like an extra in a horror film." "Maybe that is what you see, but in my mind, I put a red dress on you with heels and make up I see a princess." "Really, not a queen huh?" "No, no I mean." "It's ok I'm just funning with you Officer, Malone, that's what your name plate says right?"

"Yes Officer Darius Malone, soon to be Detective Malone granted I pass the test." "To be prepared, one must study so his knowledge can be effusive." Grinning "Well said grasshopper, here is my card, hopefully you will use it." Pausing "Only time will tell, I'll keep your number on file." Once I closed my door I exhaled a sigh of relief. I'm thinking, did he come about my life by choice or the jig was up. He is fine though but it might be a conflict of interest around me. Let me not

worry about that right now, fix me
some coffee and watch the news.

CHAPTER 3

THE SCAM

A little after one o'clock I made it to Jake's Eatery and Samara is already here. She got us a table outside so I went inside to place my order. After ten minutes I received my food and went to the table to sit with her. At first, we were eating and making small talk. Then, when were finish eating she pulls out a miniature cigar, lit it and begin to talk about what she has on her mind.

"Listen Karessa' the first scam I got is a simple one, bank fraud, making false bank statements for false bank accounts. We use client's information to create these phony accounts on paper. I have a few of my friends I know from college that works in a couple of banks. I drop the applications for these accounts off to them and they'll make bogus banking accounts in our client's names. The bank will mail a checking book and an ATM card to them. Once they received the goods they give me a call and I get in touch with my people from the bank. In two days twenty to twenty-five thousand dollars will be transferred into their account. When the money drops into their account they will get an alert from the bank about the deposit. The next day they go into the bank, withdraw all the money out of their accounts. They meet up with me, I get the cash, pay them for their services, we get our cut and the rest go to my banking friends."

Sitting and thinking to myself, that's a good plan but I found one flaw. "What if the client decides to disappear with the money Samara, get the cash and run?" Squinting her eyes she says with some attitude "They're not going to do that Karessa', we have all of their information, their personal information is more valuable than the few thousands of dollars they will receive. Go ahead, run, run far away from us, we can make credit cards in their name and that's just the beginning. Their credit line will be so messed up it will take them three consecutive life times for them to fix the problem. Do you really think they want to chance that and that's a rhetorical question?" "I never thought about that Samara, sounds like a great plan, but, why do you need me, I mean, can you do all of that yourself?" Looking at me with a blank stare "I need you to type up all of the documents that is it, I will get the clients and their info. It's not just one or two people we are dealing with for the scam I got a shit load of clients, ready to go on this.

It will be worth your while Karessa', we are going to do this for two or three months tops, once we are done my friends from the banks they're leaving the country and by the way, I need you to make them some passports. You won't be seen, I won't be seen, all of our clients bogus bank accounts will be wipe from all the computers, you make their information vanish, it's the perfect crime." It is the perfect crime and I want even have to leave my home to be involved. It didn't take me any longer to think.

"I'm in, so how much will I make off of each client's applications I do?" "Two thousand guaranteed and I got ten already to go, now do the math." "Ok, between me and the clients, that just five thousand dollars, if it's twenty, that's fifteen left, so what's your cut Samara?" Taking a pull on her cigar, blowing smoke rings in the air. "Five and the rest is theirs, does that bother you?" "Not at all sweetheart, I understand the pecking order." "Cool, I'll bring everything you will need tonight to your house if that's ok with you."

"That's perfect, by the way, you said you had a couple of things to talk to me about, what else you had to say?" Standing up, she passes me her cigar "You're right, I did ma' mi, but I spoke prematurely, once I make sure that it's a go you will be the first to know Ms. Vault, smooches." As I watched her walk away I took a pull off the cigar she gave me, finished the rest of it and went to go buy a bottle of tequila to have for later.

CHAPTER 4

BETRAYAL

Back at my apartment I was on my computer when I got a call. It's an old friend of mines from my neighborhood I grew up in. We join the gang around the same time. Went to the same school, you know, we did a few things together. He's telling me about a job he needs help with and if everything goes smooth I can have seventy-five hundred in my pocket. Ok, I can live with that, now I need to know what services I can provide to this deed.

"So, once you disable the alarm system, I'll go in and you keep watch." I'm looking at the house, scoping out the whole scenery, for all possible exits in case I had to get away. "Cool, so how much money you said that's in there?" "About thirty-thousand including some jewelry, that's a bonus." Smirking "Well, it sounds like the deal we have need to be renegotiated. Give me ten." "Ten! Are you for real Karessa'? (with a surprised look on his face.) How you going to come at me like that?" "Come at you like what, you just said it's thirty-thousand in there." "I said about thirty Karessa'." In an aggressive tone "Ok, about thirty, that still doesn't changed the fact plus jewelry Cody, damn man just hit me with a ten. Not only am I the look out, I'm the only person you know that can disarm a system and if any interruption gets in our way I shoot first, fuck the questions later. If you can find a bitch bad as me then show her to me other than that, I want ten."

Staring me in my eyes and I'm staring him back in his. "Ok Karessa', ok, you got it, now let's go get this money." Before we got out the car my phone started ringing. Damn, it's Samara, I forgot about tonight. When somebody talks money to me and about getting it right then and there that's what my mind is on. "What's up girl?" "What's up, I'm on my way to you, what's your address?" "Listen, give me about an hour, I done got myself wrapped up in a situation, once I'm done I'll call you then you can meet me at my apartment."

After a short pause "That's cool, I'll go get something to eat, don't leave me hanging." "Just one hour I promise. I'll hit your phone as soon as I'm finished, I got you."

Damn, I need that job more than this one, especially since this clown trying to stiff me on it. Let me get this over with so I can handle the business I got with Samara. I disabled the alarm system, hid in the bushes while Cody broke in through the side door. Ten minutes has gone past, he should be getting ready to show his face. After another ten minutes, I decided to go inside to see what's taking him so long. As I'm creeping around I called out his name a couple of times. About time I reach the kitchen the back door is open with a breeze blowing lightly through it. This son of a bitch left out the back door on me. He just fucked me with no Vaseline or a condom. Can't believe I trusted him, he played me real good. Cody just another problem I will have to deal with later, let me go meet Samara.

Leaving out the house a vehicle is pulling into the drive way. So I ducked back inside ran through the living room to the kitchen. Left out the back door and hopped over the fence and made it to my car. Riding back to my house to meet Samara, I called Cody phone, of course he didn't answer. I didn't leave a message because the message I have, I will deliver it personally. When I pulled up in front of my building Samara is standing out front puffing on one of her miniature cigars, drinking on a juice. "Hey chick, let's go upstairs." Walking up the stairs, she blurted out you know you got a nice ass. Caught off guard I thanked her, feeling a bit weird but at the same time flattered. When we get inside my apartment I flopped down on my couch while Samara sat on my love seat.

"What's wrong girl, you looking tired and what's up with all the black clothing, you going Goth now?" Slightly rolling my eyes at her "I had to take care of something, but it didn't turn out the way I thought it would." "I understand maybe next time chica." "Definitely the next time, you can be sure of it. What you got for me?" as I sat up on the couch. Samara gets up from the love seat and sat next to me.

"This is the moneylope, the first ten like I told you." Giggling "The moneylope huh, how cute, it looks more like a big ass yellow envelope to me." "It is, but what's inside is guaranteed money." "I see said the blind man, so when do you need this back?" "Sunday, I'm making the first drop off Monday. By the end of the week I'll bring you more clients and keep the same routine from there." "Good, good." As I shake my head. "I guess we are done here, see you Sunday, what's a good time for you Karessa'?" "Come around seven, seven thirty-ish, I'll have everything ready to go." We both stood up at the same time, Samara looking me in my face.

"Do you drink Karessa'?" Wondering should I answer the question "In fact I do, about to jump in the shower, get comfortable and sip on some tequila after you leave." "Well, that sounds like a plan, maybe Sunday when I come over we can do some shots, my treat." "Since it's your treat how could I say no, it's a date." Walking towards the door she turned around and smile. "It sure will be, looking forward to it, bye Karessa'." "See you in a minute Samara."

Closing and locking my door it seems as if my clothes just melted off me. I left a trail from the front door to my bathroom. Washing up, all I could think about is how Cody played me. Excuse my French but that was a bitch move he pulled on me. All I wanted was a fair share of the loot that's if he were telling the truth. He's going to get thirty big faces plus the jewelry and all I wanted was ten. This is the reason why I always do things solo. It's hard for me to trust people, it's no more honor amongst thieves anymore. But he's going to pay me, see this is the deal with individuals like Cody.

They are creatures of habit he's been staying in the old neighborhood and doing the same thing like forever. Where did I just pick him up from tonight, the hood in front of his house; where he still living in his grandmother's attic. He's not hard to find, not at all by a long shot. See how's he thinking, I'm looking for him right now, the thing about it is, I am. But it's going to be minimal, just to show my face here and there. It's going to get back to him that I have been looking for him.

So he's going to stay low off the radar only move around when he has to. Picking out the curtains before he steps on the concrete, screening his phone calls, tell his grandmother to tell me he's not home. But the one thing I've learned out of all things the armed service had trained me for, is patience. Wait your enemy out, no matter how long it takes, you wait before you strike. Because once you do, the blow will have to be so severe that it renders your enemy helpless. That's why Cody can hide for the next week, month or year,

but before he leaves this God giving
earth, he's going to pay me by cash
or his life.

CHAPTER 5

OFFICER MALONE

This tequila is so smooth and perfect, out of all spirits I had done tequila is my favorite. Sitting by the window with my feet hanging out, all the lights out in my apartment except for my bedroom. Just me, the stars, the moon and the street lights are the only things I want to see glowing right now. I should have gotten one of them cigars from Samara before she left, that would of help with the mood I'm in. Wouldn't you know it, I hear people yelling outside, disturbing my groove, so I get up and look out the window.

It's a crowd down the street in front of the Deli I assume it's a fight going on. And of course like clockwork here comes the screeching of the sirens and the blaring of the police lights. (Sighing) Guess I'll watch the show since it did just interrupt my meditation moment. Couldn't see too much from my window so I went down stairs and sat on the stoop. With all the commotion going on I left my drink upstairs. Damn it, the drink tasting so good too, plus, I'm beginning to feel it also if you know what I mean. As the crowd started to disperse I got up to go back inside my apartment but as I'm walking inside I hear the chirp of a police siren behind me.

"Hey pretty lady." I turned around and it's Officer Malone, smiling at me. "Hey there Officer Malone, what brings you into my neck of the woods tonight?" "Well it was a fight down the street by the deli that I got dispatch for, but I wished it were under different circumstances." Walking up to the curb "And what circumstances would you had preferred?" "If I were coming to visit a friend, more like a young lady I met a little while ago, but that couldn't be because I never got a call from her." "That's understandable, maybe the young lady has been a little busy would everything be ok if she apologizes for her actions?" "Maybe, but I think it would be more sufficient if this young lady goes out on a date with me, (Shrugging his shoulders) I'm just saying." "How about this, have a lunch date with the young lady and if everything goes well, we will see about the next episode." Shaking his head up and down in slow motion "I can take that deal, how does Wednesday sounds, around noon?" "That's perfect, I'll call you at eleven and you tell me where to meet you at." "Sounds perfect Ms. Vault, you have a peaceful night." "I'll try, but it depends on the people in my neighborhood." Laughing as he drives off, I looked around my area then went into my place.

Back in my apartment, I picked up where I left off, but thinking about dealing with a police officer. I know he can't come over here, at least not now. Besides that, being in a relationship right now isn't in my cards too. Down the line maybe, but at this moment my mind is focus on money. I'll just pray it could be what the big man up in the sky planned, to get me out of what I am doing. Yes, the sound of the city is at peace with itself again. I'm going to bed to take advantage of this serenity and rest until the morning.

CHAPTER 6

VISITING THE OLD

Starting to take care of these applications, I should be done in a couple hours if not less. Taking a break to walk to the corner store I have a taste for some dough nuts, guess my sweet tooth is kicking in. But once I left the store I had a shopping bag of food. Brought me a pack of those sweet miniature cigars that Samara likes to puff on. Speaking of Samara, she texted me on my way back to the house wanting to know could she spend the night on Sunday when she comes over.

I didn't text her back right away, I had to let that marinate for a moment, why she wants to spend a night, you coming early enough to be home at a decent time. Aw that's right, she did ask me could we take some shots of tequila when she comes over, she probably don't want to drive while intoxicated. So I texted her back and said its cool, pick up some hot wings and some beer when you're on your way, might as well get it in, I can sleep in Monday anyway. Done with all the bogus applications, it's just knocking on twelve o'clock in the afternoon. Jump in the shower, threw on some tight shorts, my tight T-shirt with the mouth that has the tongue sticking out on it and my pink flip flops.

After getting me a manicure and a pedicure, I decided to ride through the old neighborhood to make an

appearance and to let Cody know
I'm missing him, being sarcastic.
Saw some of my old buddies
standing around so I parked my car
and hung out with them for about a
couple of hours. This one guy I
used to mess around with back in
the day wasn't even a boyfriend,
calls himself trying to reminisce
about the past with me. He can stop
it because I see where's he going
with this and nothing is even
happening on that level anymore.
Then on top of that, he's looking
busted and staying at his sister and
her husband's house. How old are
you again sir, I mean, if a person
needs help that I can understand,
I've been there. But I can tell he
hasn't been doing anything with
himself. And I already got the scoop

from a few of my friends before he showed up over here. Now here's the kicker, he had one to many drinks and wants to grab and pull on me.

Telling me I think I'm better than everybody and I'm not going anywhere unless it's with him. Whoa... he must think I'm one of these half brain chicks that goes for a man putting his paws on them and does what he wants them to do, too much testosterone. The first thing I told him is please get your hands off of me Larry you're making a spectacle of yourself, plus making a scene. Trying to be polite but his testosterone wouldn't let him back down, but I can expect this, where we are from this how a man supposed to act. Or at least that's how they think, you know, for their reputation, but I wasn't too big on a person's reputation. Our people yelling at him to let me go, he's not listening to them, he is in his own little zone. I guess I'm going to have to teach him about unwanted advances, the Karessa' Vault way.

After a few more pleases and don'ts and stops; I gripped his hand and wrist then proceeded to do a three sixty under his arm and twisted it. He's facing the ground while I have his arm lifted above his body. Of course everybody's amaze, Larry's whining yelling bitch let me go. Since he wanted to use the B word in place of my name I applied more pressure to his arm. By now he has dropped down to one knee, but insisted on staying in tough mode. Some more bitch, I'm going to do this, bitch I'm going to do that made me decide to really humiliate him even more.

So I let him go, rubbing his arm and shoulder he's approaching me saying what he's going to do to me. Standing in a fighting stance he comes at me with his right fist, so predictable because I know he's a righty and his swing is weak. I ducked down, stuck my leg out and pushed him so he could trip to the ground. Everybody is laughing he's drunk face down, one of the guys lifted him up on his feet. Still wanting to fight me, enraged, I can feel the heat coming from off his body, he picks up a stick off the ground. Now everybody is trying to break it up but I tell them no, let him go. Upon releasing him, he rushes with the stick raised above his shoulder. Standing there, my mind is always five steps ahead of my opponent I knew what I was going to do to him before he made a move. I hear yelling, get out of the way is heard by one of the by standers.

I intend to get out of the way, but first I must let him get close enough. He's right where I want him. He took his swing, I jump back. Now the force of his swing made him do a one eighty. When he stopped I was already behind him with one arm around his neck, my other arm is locking my hand of the one around his neck. You guess it, time for someone to say good night. Larry is reaching behind trying to grab me by my hair. As he dropped to one knee he's whining again but his body is going limp, every attempt to grab me by my hair is useless. I just let him go and watched his body fall onto the grass. See how nice I am, I could have easily let him fall on the concrete, but I'm no monster unless you make me be. He's laid there, snoring, a couple of our friends picked him up, dragged him to his sister's house. Leaned him against the door, rang the bell and ran. We continued the festivities for another hour, but before I left since I was around the corner, I decided to knock on Cody grandmother's door to see if he's there.

No one answered, walking back to my car I turned around quick and saw the curtains in the attic moving.

Funny because no other curtains in the house are moving and it's no wind blowing and all the windows are closed. I know it's Cody he will get more than a sleeper hold when I'm finished with him. He will wish that move he did on me would had never crossed his mind, ever.

CHAPTER 7

CURIOSITY

Tipsy, I'm back in my neighborhood, but not before I grab me a bite to eat from the neighborhood restaurant. Once I cross my threshold, all my windows are open from earlier and I took all my clothes off except my panties, hey, I have to leave a little to the imagination incase a peeping Tom wants to peek at me from the building across the street. Just feeling so sexy right now, not bragging but putting that asshole to sleep really has my blood pumping. I never did it before just practice it when I was in the services. So for it to work the first time I tried it makes a woman feel good about herself.

Eating just half of the food I brought the rest I put in the refrigerator for later. Turning off the lights, I went and stood in front of my window posing like someone's painting me puffing on my cigar. Feeling kind of horny with no man on my list to call, guess I'll have to pleasure myself. Aw, now that I released my stress I fell asleep, only to be waking in the morning by a car accident. Is it me or some shit happens around here like clockwork. But I'm glad I'm woke, I needed to double and triple check the phony applications to make sure everything is correct and ready for Samara to take with her tonight.

Damn I forgot, she's spending the night, let me remind her to bring them hot wings and beer I asked her to bring. Walking into the living room picking up the envelope by the computer I flopped down on the couch and then text Samara. Agreeing to what I asked her for, I finished up checking the bogus applications but man I'm hungry. Looking in the refrigerator trying to persuade myself to finish off the meal I brought last night, I'm more in a sandwich and chips type of mood. Light eating, but tonight I will feast laughing to myself. Once the day begin to entertain the night, the sun begin to do a disappearing act, I took a soak in the tub for an hour.

It's a knock at my front door, so I put my robe on and looked through the peep hole. "Who is it?" I asked. "Your next door neighbor." she replied. Cracking open my door, she says "Hi my name is Dorothy sorry to disturb you, but can I borrow some sugar?" Puzzle by the request because no one ever knocks on my door, especially anyone that lives in this building. "Sure Dorothy." I took her bowl and returned it to her with sugar in it. Reaching my hand out the door, "Here you go." she replied "Thank you I didn't catch your name." I said "Because, I never threw it, (we both laughed) my name is Karessa'."

"What a pretty name, Karessa', I like that." "Well thank you

Dorothy, what apartment you stay in again?" "Apartment 2D, right next door, I've seen you in and out at times." "Oh really, so are you the neighborhood watch captain?" "Oh no, just don't go out much, unless I have to, I'm a loner, no boyfriend, no family, just me." Wondering why she's disclosing her personal life to me. "Ok, well maybe I will see you again but right now, I need to get ready." With my finger I motion it, up and down my robe. "Aw ok, sorry and thank you again, maybe we will you never know."

Before closing my door I watched her to see if she were going to 2D. As she walked inside she turns my way and waved at me. I smiled, waved back then shut my door. Getting dress it still feel kind a strange that I'm in 2A and she skipped two apartments to knock on my door. Maybe the people who occupy those apartments weren't home or she was just being nosy. I'll have to keep an eye out on her. I know, I'll invite her over one day get some information out of her without her knowing she is volunteering it. Put her in my mental note for later; now let me get ready before Samara gets here.

I straighten up my apartment, put all the applications back in the envelope then sat looking out the window wondering is something going to happen tonight. Hey, I'm on my way and I got what you have asked me to pick up is the text I just got from Samara. Ok, I'm here waiting on you I replied back. Oh it feels so good getting my hands and nails done. Twenty-five minutes later Samara is knocking at my door. After I opened the door to let her in with a bit of shock I'm surprised on what she is wearing. "Girl, you looking like you're about to hit the club and shake some ass." "Nah chica I had to attend this event earlier today, I was going to go home and change but changed my mind." as she smiled. "Well you look hot, if I were a man I'll be trying to get you to come over tonight." "Karessa' quit playing, I got my emergency shorts and tank top I keep in my trunk in my bag, do you mind if I jump in the shower right quick, I do feel a little, dirty." "Um, no, go right ahead, towels in the closet and extra tooth brushes if you need one. Do you need lotion and deodorant?" Looking offended "No, I have that covered, but thank you anyway, could you put the beer in the fridge for us I hate warm beer." "Sure, I'll put it in the freezer so it can get a quick chill, anything else you need princess?" "No, well, I might need you to rub lotion on my back if you don't mind." "It's cool, just let me know, I'll be right here."

She went to take her shower, I lit me a cigar and cracked open a beer. I gave my parents a call and my father answered the phone. My mother was sleep so we chatted for about fifteen minutes, I love my dad he's a straight to the point type of guy. I always got to give sometime between talking to them because my father told me, don't call every week, we don't have anything to talk about every week. Just check in once a month that will give us time for something to build up and talk about. He's a character, the only other time to call before a month's spacing is if it's an emergency. But I'm going this week to see them, haven't seen them in a while. And I just might spend the night, my mother will love it, him, he'll love it too, talk trash, but love every minute of it.

Now, what are these fools up to? Looking out my window, I see about seven boys and two girls walking pass my building. Loud and moving like their anxious to get to whatever trouble that awaits them. Let me not judge a book by its cover, they might be on their way to go play some basketball or sing some Christmas carols. Wishful thinking I guess and look who's finally coming out of the shower. Samara steps in the living room with her dry towel wrapped around her body. "I see you started the party without me, did I take too long?" "Of course you didn't, I just had a beer that's all." "I smell the sweet aroma of a cigar too." "I see nothing get pass you, tell me what I'm thinking now." As she use her hands to open up her towel. "If I tell you what you are thinking, I wouldn't be in this towel right now, now would I." Samara went to the back to get dressed, I pondered on this brief conversation we just had. What would make her think I would be thinking what she just said I was thinking? The bad thing about it is, I didn't even reply back to what she said. Now it got me second guessing myself. I never in my life ever desired to be with another woman, but woman have come on to me before. And I set them straight, hmm, somehow though, I am somewhat curious. What am I saying, hell no, I love men, let me think about something else.

By then, Samara came back into the living room. She had on the tightest shorts and a tank top that could barely lock down them beach balls she calls breast. She went to the refrigerator to get her a beer, walked and sat on the couch. The way she's sitting is making it hard for me not to think about her in a sexual manor. I got up and grab the tequila, a couple of shot glasses, lime and salt. As I'm motioning towards the couch Samara is locked on me, her eyes going up and down like an elevator. I'm feeling somewhat nervous and just a bit uncomfortable. She lifts her legs to place her feet on the floor so I could sit next to her. Putting the drink and the rest of what I was carrying on the table the salt box tipped over. We both reach at it to sit it up at the same time with her hand touching the top of mines. I looked at her and smiled then apologize like I did something wrong. She said no need to apologize our instincts just kicked in and made us react at the same time.

Once the salt box was upright I sat down on the couch.

"Are you alright Karessa', you seem somewhat tense." "I'm good, just had a moment that's all, could you pass me that box of cigars?" She reached onto the table to pick up the cigars, passing them to me she says "With that being said, let's get those shots going, I'm ready to get tipsy." Sounding surprised "Just tipsy, I thought you wanted to party?" "I do girl, tipsy is an understatement, put some music on and have some fun." I went to my computer while Samara poured us some shots. We took the first one and it kicked me in my chest like a mule. But I'm ready for my next one. About time we got to our six shot and a couple of beers, we're in the middle of the floor singing and dancing. Loud enough that the neighbor under me took a broom handle to their ceiling for us to cut down the noise. Not needing any unwanted attention we turned the music down, heated up the hot wings and got our grub on. Finishing off those wings, it's time for some more shots, when I reached the third one, I was done. Leaning back puffing away on my cigar taking occasional sips of my beer you could knock me down with a feather. Samara started laughing out of nowhere, hysterically. With her laughing it begun to make me laugh and I don't even know what I'm laughing for.

Totally under the influence of the spirits, I didn't notice that Samara had laid her legs in my lap. "So, are you ready to make some money Karessa'?" Half slurring "Yes I am, got the applications ready, now let's get paid." "This just the beginning baby, I got other hustles I am working on, stick with me and you will be bleeding green blood." As she lean back on the couch fiddling her feet together. "I'm with you girl, just don't cross me, don't ever betray my trust." Taking a pull off her cigar "You don't have to worry about that, I am the same way, it's a few lames I had to put out of my circle, had them deep in my pockets, but they won't be able to do that to anybody no more." "I feel you on that, had to do what you had to do, it happens at time." "These people we are doing this job with at the bank, how well do you know them?" Looking up into space "Two of them I know pretty well, we have done things together before, penitentiary type of things understand me. Now the third guy, that's one of their friends I met once, when they came to me about this plan." "What kind of vibe did you get from her?" "It's not a woman it's a male and he seems ok to me, I didn't get any bad vibes, he actually called himself trying to hit on me on the sly." "Well you're a nice looking chick Samara." Smiling firmly "Am I, thank you Karessa', you're not bad yourself. Are you into women Ms. Vault?" "I have never been with a woman." "That's not what I asked you, I asked you are you into women Ms. Vault."

Taking a sip of my beer "Are you inferring that I like women?" "I never inference anything, does the question makes you uncomfortable?" "No, look, I've never been with a woman in that way, but I have been somewhat curious. What about you Samara?" "Yes I have (Confidently saying), a couple of times during college, one time in high school." Sounding curious "Did you enjoy a woman putting her lips all over you?" "To tell you the truth, I did enjoy it, well I do enjoy it, far as being in a relationship with a woman, I don't know about that." "Hmm."
"What?" "It's nothing." "No, no, tell me, what's brewing in the mind of Karessa'." "It's nothing, really."

Samara started motioning slowly towards me, talking in a low sexy voice. "I know what's on your mind missy. You are wondering, how is it to have sex with a woman, a particular one name Samara. That compliment I made about your ass the other day stuck in that pretty little mind of yours. Aw yea, I have been watching you since the first day I saw you. But I couldn't get a good read on you. I admit, I was somewhat intimidated by you, the rough edge you have about yourself. Your intelligence is vigorous, your beauty is overwhelming plus you got one hell of a body. I consider you dangerous to a fault, everything must happen your way, you must be in control." (Sitting on my lap facing me) But you don't mind if someone takes the lead in the bedroom. As long as that someone knows what they are doing. You're also mysterious a person could be close to you but still won't know everything about you. That's what makes Karessa' such a hot catch. Are you wondering do the juices in my mouth get warm once I'm turned on? How juicy Samara gets when I'm touched in the right places. It's only one way to find this out, do you want to find out?" Swallowing the saliva that Samara just made me produced in my mouth "Yes, I guess I do."

We begin to kiss, from there, the kissing got more passionate. She is right I like to be controlled by my partner in bed. I control everything else in my life. The money I make, all the moves I do. I have been like that since I was a young girl. No one can get over on me, if they do, that's a sign a weakness to me. The service didn't do anything but fuel that desire I have for being the strongest. So yes, I would like one thing in m,y life I couldn't or don't have to control. I can, I just don't want to, tell me what to do. Pleasure me for once I give you the permission to do whatever you want me to do. By now Samara is licking, sucking and fondling my breast. That's what I want, squeeze them as hard as you want, I will not scream, I promise. Treat me like the tramp I am, use my body for your amusement. I can handle any punishment you dish out, I'm a big girl I love pain.

Now she's kissing down my
stomach, twirling her tongue around
in my navel. Feeling like she is
French kissing me down there.
Every fiber of my being is jumping.
I took my hands, reached over my
shoulders and grabbed the sofa.
This is definitely not her first time
with a woman each contact with my
skin makes my pearl tongue tingle.
Oh my, she's taking my thighs for a
thrill. Her soft lips are making wet
smacking sounds, once she finish
biting down on my flesh then
pulling back and letting go. The
only light that is on is my desk lamp.
Casting our shadows on the wall,
where if somebody wanted to see
our show they could get it for free.
I'm not a shame and I don't care, let
them lust, that just makes what she's

doing to me more stimulating. I know Samara pussy is pulsating it got to be. Taking my shorts off bending me over on the couch sliding my thong string over and keeping it in place with her thumb. She takes my ass and play with it on her slippery tongue. Trying not to be loud I let out a few low moans. As her face is between my butt cheeks she guided two of her fingers inside me. That's when the build up inside me commence to erupt, next thing I know I'm squirting all over her hands and my sofa. This never happened to me before, when she pulled her fingers out, I was done. Stuck in the position she had me in I could hear her sucking on her fingers pleasured by the outcome.

Smacking me on my ass, she laughed lightly and pushes me down. Kissing me then she stopped. "Was that fantastic for you, because it was phenomenal for me." Laid in my own juices "It was epic but I have a secret to tell you." "What you got to tell me?" "I never in my life ever squirted before. The way it felt is so hard to describe, but I can say I want to feel that way again." Laughing "Well I'm glad you enjoyed it, I aim to please and you tasted every bit that I thought you would." Samara climb on the couch behind me, hugging me "Karessa' what we just shared is a beautiful thing, I don't want this to affect our friendship in anyway." "I hear you, it want, this here is just a benefit package that comes along with the job." "Right and this help our bond grow stronger, more on some sisterhood thing you know it's ok to have a few perks."

CHAPTER 8

I'M IN

"You know what Samara, you never did tell me about this other job, the one you mentioned at the lunch spot that day." "Wow, look at you, I guess good sex doesn't affect you for long, you're right back to business." "It's just been on my mind on and off, since it popped back in my cranium again I thought I would ask before it slips out of my mind again. Did I offend you about asking that question?" Twisting my hair between her fingers "No baby, I just needed some more time before I explain it all but I can tell you the sketch of it.

It's this woman I know, I met her
through a friend, a wealthy
individual, well not wealthy but it
would take decades for her to
become broke. Her and my friend
were dating which turned into a
relationship, they almost got
married. He didn't know her and I
was having sex behind his back, to
tell you the truth as freaky as he is,
he would probably get mad because
we didn't let him participate. Any
who, at times that I was with her she
took me on trips to a few shing
dings, some extravagant, some so-so.
Pillow talking she told me about this
diamond she has worth between
seventy-five to one hundred
thousand dollars. It's kept in a safe
downtown at The Pentecostal bank,

where the rich in this city keep a lot of their valuables.

One day I went to the bank just to see their policies and bullshit, gather information basically. (Now we are both sitting upright on the couch.) The policy of putting things in and taking them out is an **ID** and signature. This is the most beautiful thing about it the bank never seen her before. The only thing they know is her race." Interrupting her "Her race, I don't get it, how they never seen her before?" "Because she did transactions when she was living in Africa, she got it at an auction here in the United States. One of the persons she has working for her went to the auction for her and got the diamond. He did all the footwork, if she wants it she just go to the bank, produce her ID and sign her signature, that's it." With a confused look on my face "Ok, what does that have to do with me?"

"You can be her, make a fake identification, sign her name and walk out with the diamond." My head slightly leaning "Are you crazy, how can you expect me to pull that off?" "Look Karessa', you are about her height, same body type, they never seen her before baby, I'm telling you we can get away with this." "I don't know give me some time to think about this." "Seriously, we need to activate this plan immediately this is the perfect time to strike, next time I go to see her I'm getting her information, you need to let me know are you in or out." Samara gets up, lit her cigar and grabbed a beer then sat at the window. I stayed on the sofa for a few more minutes, contemplating on this scam Samara just brought to me. I can see she's upset about what I said but this my life on the line and it might not go as well as she thinks.

After going to the bathroom and taking a hoe bath I put my T-shirt on. Going over to her I put my hands on her shoulders and massage them slowly. "Ok, I'm in, let's do it." "Are you sure, I don't want to pressure you." "Yes, you better be sure about the bank never seeing her and get any information on her, her social, birth certificate what soda she likes." "I'm one hundred percent, but I'll triple check, hey, I won't send you on a bogus job baby, I need you more than you need me and I will gather all her information just in case." Hugging in front of the window and kissing, a man yelled from the street can I come up there with y'all. We said no at the same time as we were laughing at his advances.

In the morning Samara hops out the bed and jumps in the shower to get ready to go drop off the paperwork to her banking friends. I got some passports I got to do but pretty much my day is free. Put my robe on and went to check my mailbox since I haven't checked it in some days. Going back up Dorothy is coming down the stairs and she's accompanied by a man. We made small talk and she introduced me to him, kind of looks like a federal agent to me. His suit is nice, manicured nails, hairline is extra crisp, shoes and watch looks about it cost him fifteen, sixteen hundred.

I know, I'm very observant and I guarantee I'm at least ninety five percent right about this guy. The way she's dress doesn't compliment his style. Her sun dress and heels looks cheap, the pearls aren't helping and for the love of clowns she has on too much make up. Judging by her appearance, not knocking her but I believe Dorothy is a prostitute. That's none of my business, if that is what she chose to make money I'm not one to talk. Because I'm not laying on my back for it but I am still on the same side of the law she is on.

Going back inside my apartment Samara is sitting at my kitchen table putting her shoes on. Upon leaving, she tells me I want hear from her until the end of the week. It's a lot of things that she has to take care of one of them is getting the information of her rich friend. "Take your time." is what I told her. "Don't rush it everything needs to be precise so it can be a clean get away." She gave me a kiss and proceeded out the door.

CHAPTER 9

THE ENCOUNTER

Feeling groggy because I didn't have an ounce of sleep, like a magnet my bed pulled me back to it, picking up my watch off the night stand its twelve o'clock on the head. Even though it seems later than what it is I missed a couple of calls. Nobody important, my body needs a pick me up I see a cup of coffee on the horizon. I wanted some good java from the shop, cleaning myself up I left out the door.

Walking to my car I see a piece of paper or a flyer on my windshield. It wasn't neither it's a ticket. Damn, for street cleaning, this is some bullshit. Where are the signs, there's a couple of signs on the street light pole ten feet down. Wouldn't you know it, in fine print this is one of the days the city cleans this side of the street. This place I swear, nick pick for every little dollar they can take from us. Getting over this ticket crisis; now I can go have my date with a cup of coffee. The coffee shop is packed with a bunch of office cubicle yuppies. Young and old, I was going to sit outside at one of their tables but I'll go for a stroll once I get it. Strolling down past the clothing store I see my old buddy Sergeant Moroza from the Marines. Look at him sitting on his motor cycle with all that leather on. He's actually the person who taught me about making fake ID's and other things. I'm going to sneak up behind him and surprise him. Once I did my little surprise attack he jump, turned around and smiled.

He hopped off his bike picking me up as he hugged me, after putting down he stepped back with his arms open in a gesture of surprise about seeing me. After the how you been, blah, blah, blah talk, he said he's in the city until next Monday. He's handling some business right now and he lives an hour away from the city out in the suburbs. In the middle of our conversation he asked me are you still doing bump jobs as he calls them. Yes I replied, trying to learn more hustles to add on to my resume. Putting my number in his phone he then called my phone so I can save his number in mines.

"I got some things brewing, big dollars to be made, if you don't mind the risk, when it's time I'll call you and we can talk some more," he said. "Cool, if it makes dollars it makes sense to Karessa'." I told him. He told me "By the way leave the Serge stuff back with the services, call me Fernando, we're friends ma." Laughing in my imitation Spanish voice I said "Ok poppy, I will call you Fernando for now on." He smiled, skidded off on his motor cycle throwing me the peace sign.

That's what I like more work, I need money coming in constantly. I didn't even have to touch my savings, just adding to it so it can grow. Tuesday night I got a text from Fernando flirting with me. I flirted back I'm not going to lie, he got this Amaury Nolasco look about him, you know the fine guy from prison break. While we are texting back and forth I get another text on my phone. Officer Darius Malone reminding me about our lunch date we have tomorrow. I'm glad he did because I really did forget about it. Thanks for reminding me, even though I remembered I texted him back. I know I'm lying but what he doesn't know won't hurt him. Right now I'm tired and ready for dream land. I bid Fernando a good night and let the calm of the night take me to my destination, sleep.

I showed up late for our date on purpose, to see if he would say anything about it. But I got no reaction from it, he is just happy I showed up I guess. The date started off a little stale but beyond more of the conversation we found out we got some things in common. He did ask me what I do for a living. Pausing I said, "I'm a self-employed investor I play the market and handle other people's money in the stock market." "That's a nice profession he says, maybe you can do some investing for me sometime." "Maybe." I stuffed my mouth full of the salad not making any eye contact. Asking me how I feel about police, "I told him I'm not a big fan.

I use to get harass by them in my old neighborhood where I grew up. It's understandable, it was crime happening there but to think everyone is a criminal and stop them for no probable cause is ridiculous." Shaking his head "I can see where you're coming from, that would not make me trust law enforcement as much either." "But you seems like one of the good apples out of the batch, am I right Darius?" "Yes you are I believe in the oath that I took, I try to treat every citizen the same, no matter what the situation may be." "You try huh, doesn't sound like you put a lot of effort in your work." Looking puzzled "What I mean by try Karessa' is that, I try to treat each citizen the same, but some citizens no matter how nice I am to them still want to push the envelope and test my kindness. That's why I said try I give everyone the benefit of the doubt I come in contact with, that is what an officer supposed to do. But some people like the hard way out rather than take the easy road I lay out for them."

Leaning back from the table "I can see somebody is passionate about their job, I didn't mean to ruffle your feathers, officer." "Don't worry you didn't, that's how deep I am when it comes to this job, everybody should be passionate or somewhat if what they chose to do in life is something they love, do you agree?" "You are preaching to the choir." As I take a drink of my beverage. "So, why isn't a guy like you married, you seem like a nice catch, I don't know everything about you but I'm usually a good judge of character. You're a hot commodity, intelligent and not trying to inflate your ego, charming and sexy." Blushing "First off thank you for the compliments and I was almost married once about five years ago.

She was beautiful too, frizzy hair, full set of lips, slanted green eyes, golden brown skin with the grace of a panther. Her name is Puhnee from the Caribbean Islands. Moved to the states in her teen years, family is well off. We met at a night club, some drunk was harassing her so I stepped in, he took a swing at me and I put him in his place. After that we dated for two years, I loved her so much I popped the question.

(With grief in his face) She told her father, he told her she cannot marry me, said I were a low life police officer, a peasant in his eyes. How I didn't have any money plus my color didn't match his criteria of the man he saw his daughter to spend the rest of her life with." "Wow, what did she say?"

"She didn't want to lose her inheritance, so she sided with daddy my love for her wasn't strong enough to change her mind." "I'm sorry to hear that Darius." "Thanks, so what about you, why haven't some young stallion tied you down." "I'm not ready to get married yet I'm not where I want to be, I want to be comfortable. What I mean is, I just want all my business in order, I can deal with seeing someone, you know. It will take more than two years before I agree to get married though. (With a slight laugh) I'm still young, but I do want some kids one day, I'll take one boy and one girl, the best of both worlds as I see it. Let me stop talking, I'm not the marrying type." "Why would you say that, as beautiful as you are any man would die to have you on their arm Karessa'." "Stop making me blush, you're not going to get any extra points for that." "This is not a basketball game so I'm not trying to, you are a catch, when you open your door that day I was astonished for real. You're gorgeous and you don't even know it."

About time we finished our lunch date, it turned into a dinner date. I'm having a great time with Darius he's cooler than I thought. Nothing but police work is what I thought he'll be talking about. But he's a worldly guy, got a hell of lot of intelligence. We ended up inside an upscale bar luckily I wore a sun dress today instead of shorts I blended right in. Taking a few shots, dancing to some good music and this place, I need to get out more, seriously. The date ended on a good note with him taking me back to my car and I gave him a hug. Driving home I thought about the ticket I got earlier and wondering could Darius do something about it. Like make it disappear laughing to myself, I doubt it watching too much television.

CHAPTER 10

EXPECT THE UNEXPECTED

When Friday rolled around, I woke up like it was Christmas. It's pay day, make around a good eighteen to twenty thousand for a few hours of work, now I know how lawyers feel. Ten of it automatically goes into my savings, pay three months of my rent, pay some bills and the rest is pocket change. Yay me, this weekend I'm going to take myself on a mini vacation. No, I'm going to rent a hotel room down town. And pamper myself, mud bath, massage, a sauna, whatever they got to offer to relax my body I'm doing it. Hey you, meeting the clients at three today, when I'm finish with them I'll be heading to you first before I hit our bank people. Samara just texted me this, that's cool, I'll be here I texted back. All fuck I said I were going to surprise my parents this weekend. I like to do what I said I am going to do. Its ok I can have fun with my parents take them out somewhere. Get them out the house for once let me give them a call. Isn't that nothing, my mother said we already got plans for the weekend, her and my father is going to their church function in San Diego and want be back until Monday afternoon. Well this sucks, I really wanted to spend some time with them. Go have fun at your stupid church thingy, I'll go with my original plan.

I booked me a room and did everything I said I was going to do,

even some extras. This weekend
was much needed, my phone been
ringing too and I didn't even answer
it. If it wasn't my parents calling
everybody else had to catch me that
Monday. I got my nails and feet
done, did a little something to my
hair feeling and looking like a movie
star. Fresh off the line with that
Mercedes Benz look and the best
thing about it, I didn't even drive I
taxi here and taxi home. While the
final hours of my get away were
winding down I decided to check
my voicemail. Out of all the
voicemails left it's one in particular
that caught my attention.

It's from Fernando saying he been
trying to reach me all weekend, he
got some work for me call ASAP. I
called him and he asked me where

am I at? Once I told him; he asked how long would it take for me to get home. He wants to pick me up because the job he got planned is on the west side of town. Feeling so lady like I really didn't want to do anything but go home and put on some lingerie and be with myself. But when money calls it's really no choice for me. Especially if I want to maintain the life style I'm living. As the taxi is pulling up in front of my building, it's a black car I've never seen before parked in front of my car. After getting out of the taxi and grabbing my bags, as I'm walking towards the entrance of the building I hear somebody whistle. I turned and look its Fernando, "Yo' hurry up ma' and change so we can go." I hustled up the stairs and did a wonder woman move. Well it felt that way. Wrapping a scarf around my head to keep my hair looking good, hopefully I don't do any sweating. As I was about to leave out the door I had to hit the bathroom. A minor delay then I hit the stairs to go down and jumped in the car and he sped off.

While we're riding he's telling me about the plot. It's an armor truck that makes a late night drop at this bank. He got an inside tip from a buddy who works for the company. The reason for the late drop off, the bank is in an undesirable area. Assuming this will be best suited for bank, not seeing any drop offs or pickups doing the hours when most people are out and about. In other words, it wouldn't be no temptation to plot and rob something you never see. Besides it's a small bank, this is the only time the armor truck comes either to pick up or drop off but tonight they are coming to drop. They come at midnight on the dot and have the keys to enter the bank. We are running behind because its eleven thirty and we must make it to the west side in twenty minutes to set up before the truck arrives. We're driving fast but not enough to arouse suspicion from the police so they would stop us. Luckily the streets are not full of vehicles it would have been difficult to maneuver. I'm a little nervous because we had a few close calls making sharp turns not knowing somebody crossing in the middle of the street.

Driving up to the bank it's about three minutes before the armor truck arrives. Not much time to come up with another plan so we decided to wing it. Pulling our ski masks down over our faces I ran and hid behind a garbage can. He secured himself inside of a door entrance that had a dim light bulb hanging over it. Really it's no need for it because it is still dark but it's perfect for a criminal.

Before I can blow on my hands to keep them warm I can hear the armor truck coming down the alley. So I took a peek and it's slowing down in front of the bank's door. Not knowing what Fernando has going through his mind I'm going to play it by ear. As I'm watching, the passenger jumps out and the driver stays in his seat. While the guard is walking to the back of the truck the driver turns off the ignition and goes over to the bank's door to open it. The guard inside the back of the truck with the cash hops out with four money bags in his hands. When he walks on the side of the truck towards the bank's door I see Fernando making his move with the grace of a cat on the same side as the guard.

That's when I came around the front of the truck to the side where everybody's at. Fernando has his gun drawn on both of the guards demanding them to go inside the bank. Forcing them inside he orders the one holding the money bags to drop them. He picks up two and I picked up the other two. We are going to lock them in the back Fernando says. He shoves one of the guards on his back to make him move in the direction he wanted him to go. The guard he pushed turns around quicker than a squad car dispatching for shots fired and grabs Fernando by his wrist making him raise his arm in the air with the gun. He drops the money bags and now they are tussling. Without even thinking the other guard made a move to help his partner, next thing I know, **BANG!** I shot him in his throat, blood gushing out the ceiling of his neck like a broken fire hydrant.

That startled his partner at which time Fernando knocks him out with his gun. Standing in shock Fernando picks up the bags and yelled let's go. Walking backwards for a second, I then turned around and ran out the door.

Running to our getaway car I hear someone yelling hey I see you. While he's starting up the car I looked out the window and see some guy on his phone. I know he's talking to 911 and giving them a description of the vehicle. Fernando pulls off so fast that the tires were screeching and left track marks in the street. After about the fourth light a police siren is blaring in the distance. Nervous, I started yelling drive faster motherfucker. We made a right heading towards the expressway. As we got close to it another police car came out of nowhere, sliding as it turns in the direction we are going. Damn, feeling nauseous as if this is a bad dream, I just wanted to get away.

We get on the expressway but Fernando pulls right back off at the next exit. The police are on our ass but after a couple blocks Fernando loses him and pulls inside an alley. "Look get out, I'm going to distract them, you take the money and get home the best way you can, I'll call you later." he said. Doing what he said I hid in the alley down a stair case that lead to some back door. Peeking over the concrete I watched him drive out the alley onto the street. Now sirens are coming from each and every way. Looking up to the sky I ask the good Lord to forgive me and guide me home safely. Once I didn't hear any more noise from the police I came up from my hiding spot.

Looking inside a garbage can, I found a shopping bag. Dumped the garbage out of it and put the money bags in it. Threw my ski mask away and turned my shirt inside out. Fluff my hair up, left out the alley and called Samara. Sounding slightly frantic "Hey girl, I need a favor from you." I said. "What's up ma', are you alright Karessa'?" "Not really, just listen could you pick me up and drop me off at home, it's a long story?"

I told her my location and she picked me up within thirty minutes. On the way to my apartment I told her what happened. Inside my home I'm still visibly shaking but feeling more comfortable inside my own space. Pouring me some tequila I then sat at my kitchen table and put my forehead in the palm of my hand. "What the hell just went down at that bank?" I'm thinking we were going to be in and out without any problems.

"Look, you always got to expect the worst case scenario when robbing someone Karessa'. That's the game we play, we want everything to go smooth; hell I even prayed that everything goes smooth. But something's you just can't control." Shaking my head "You're right, if I didn't do anything Fernando could have been dead. I never killed anyone before Samara, I know I'm capable, it just got me filling empty inside." "Here smoke some of this and take your mind off of it." Standing in front of my window blowing out a cloud of smoke, I haven't even thought about the cash we got. That's how I know my mind was somewhere else. I can smell money when it's in the vicinity but this really got me down. "Look Karessa' it's late and I got to get up early to handle some business. Are you going to be alright, you not suicidal or anything are you?" as she giggled. "No Samara, (As I laugh) you sure you don't want to spend a night?" "Not tonight cutie pie, I need to be at my home base to handle this, maybe this weekend coming up." "Ok, be careful driving home." "Also Karessa' I'm going to need that paperwork for our clients." "I'll call you later on today once I'm done with them."

I walked her to her car and she gave me a kiss on my lips. Back in my apartment I couldn't stop thinking about murdering that security guard. The blood flowing out of his neck and that confused look on his face as he felled to the floor. Speaking of which, I wonder did Fernando get away.

CHAPTER 11

YOU HAVE A PROBLEM?

Tired from all the excitement from the night I went and laid down on my couch. Staring at the ceiling, dead silence took over as I shift positions trying to get comfortable. The shopping bag with the money bags in it is on my coffee table blocking my view. The next thing I know, I'm waking up and the sun is spreading it rays throughout my field of vision. Sitting up and stretching, I picked up my phone to check the time. 9:47am, damn, it feels like I've been sleeping for a week. But it only been for some hours, I need a B12 shot. I started thinking about last night again, so I turn on my laptop to check out the local news to see if the murder made it on there.

Sure enough, it's not just in the news it's the top story. As I'm watching the news feed, they said the one witness said he saw two suspicious people running to a darken car with bags in their hands but no assailants are in custody. That means Fernando must have gotten away, but how? Half of the police force was chasing him and they were everywhere. A mouse would have been trap with nowhere to go. Rubbing my eyes, I reached over and pulled the shopping bag off the coffee table. I wasn't about to count the cash, I just wanted to see all the hundreds inside the bags. The first two I looked in were beautiful, nothing but the cold color of green filled to the capacity. When I open up the third bag, it didn't have any currency inside it. As my eyes lit up and I could see the reflection of my face in the objects, it contained one of the most precious elements on this earth. My God, diamonds, not just diamonds but a shit load of them. It felt like my heart has stopped, my mouth was watery and I couldn't shut my eye lids.

I started looking around like a prisoner eating lunch trying to guard his plate. So I took the shopping bag inside my bed room. Once I sat on my bed I poured the bag with the diamonds in it on the bed. It's about four to five nice size diamonds with at the least fifty to hundred smaller stones. I took one of the bigger ones and held it up to the sun light. The light has it glistering, like a million eyes painted on my walls.

Is someone knocking at my door? I flipped my bed cover over the diamonds, picked up my gun and approached my door. Another few knocks are heard before I reached it. "Who is it?" I asked, while holding my gun up and taking it off the safety. "Hey girl it's me, Dorothy." I asked "Dorothy?" "Yes, your next door neighbor from down the hall." Putting my gun back on safety I told her to wait a minute. I stuff the metal between the couch pillows, made sure I closed my bed room door and cracked open my front door. "Dorothy, what's up?" "Nothing much, just needed to ask you for a small favor if you don't mind." Pausing for a second "Well, I usually don't do favors on Tuesdays so it depends on what it is." Laughing she says "Karessa' you're crazy girl, it's just a small favor until Friday." "What is it?" "Can I borrow fifty dollars?" Usually I don't ask anyone who borrows money from me what is it for. Because that's not my business, just as long you pay me back. But since I don't know her that well and she even had the nerves to knock on my door to present this question, I was intrigued to ask. "What for Ms. Dorothy?" And besides I'm being nosy, I don't know what the hell she does for a living and maybe her answer will give me some idea of her profession or whatever category she fits in. "Aw honey, I got some bills and things I need to take care of but if you can, could you make it an even hundred?" No she didn't up the ante on me, the audacity of some people. It's not about the money because I could loan her a thousand dollars if I wanted to, it's the fact you barely and I do mean barely know me. I knew when I gave her some sugar that day she will be knocking on my door again one day. I know her type, my neighborhood that I am from are full of them.

Befriend you not because you are a genuine person, it's because they know when every other avenue of theirs failed to achieve their objective you're their ace in the hole. But really, I'm complaining to myself but I really don't mind helping people, just don't try to play me you know mess with my intelligence.

  "Sure, I can make it an even hundred, are you sure that's all that you need?" Looking a bit confused "Yes Karessa' but thanks for the gesture." Closing my door I go inside my purse and retrieve the money for Dorothy. "Here you go Dorothy." "Thank you so much Karessa', I will give it back to you Friday, I promise but um, all you got is a solid hundred no loose dollars." She got some nerves. "Um Dorothy, how about I take that back and you can be back at zero (I reach for the money as she snatches it away) Ok then, you don't have to make a promise, just keep your

word that goes a long way with me."
"Ok, once again thank you." As I'm
closing my door I thought I heard
her mumbling under her breath. So
I snatched my door back open.
"Did you say something?" Turning
half way around as she kept walking
"No honey, just talking to myself,
hopefully I don't answer back." I
watched her walk for a few seconds
then I close my door.

Back in my bed room I pulled my
bed cover off the diamonds. How in
the hell I'm going to get rid of
these? I don't even know where to
start, I could call Samara but could I
trust her enough to not try and
screw me over? I know she
probably got some connect with
someone in this field. While I'm
thinking I need to give Fernando a

call. I called but didn't get any answer and his voice mail box is full. Well I'll just text him, maybe he will respond.

Thursday afternoon while I'm out doing some shopping I get a text message. Its Fernando saying he needs to meet up with me, I already know what it's about. I told him to come to my apartment tonight at seven. Remind you, I haven't even counted the money yet since I saw the diamonds that's the only thing on my mind. I put the diamonds and the money bags in my safe that's in my closet. It's seven o' clock on the head and like just clockwork Fernando text me asking for my apartment number. After receiving my answer, I hear him knocking on my door. I put the bags

on my kitchen table so that's where
we sat. We chatted for a few
minutes then I had to ask, how did
you get away?

"Easily, they had nothing on me, I
gave you my mask and my gun; by
the way I will love to have back.
They hit me with evading the police,
so I got a court date coming up next
month." I said "Wow, did they ask
you why you run?" Smiling "Of
course they did, I was scared, what
else could I tell them. I'm Spanish, I
don't know, you probably thought I
was here illegally." (As he chuckled)
Don't worry Karessa', I didn't snitch
on you if that's what you are
thinking." "No I'm not thinking
that, that's the furthest thing from
my mind, I'm just glad you're ok."
"Cool, so how much did we get, I

know you counted the money." "I haven't." As I point to the money bag closes to him "Open that bag up, we got us a little bonus."

Bringing the bag towards him, he's looking at me with a big question mark on his face. "Are you fucking kidding me," he says once he looks inside. "Are these diamonds?" "Well it's not moon rocks." We both started laughing at what I just said. He's gripping them in his hands like a king holds a turkey leg. Examining each angle and inch of it, I can see the diamond's images in his eyes. "I can see why you haven't counted the money yet, these things are so mesmerizing. We should count the money though, see how much we got." "Ok, well put the rocks down and let's get our hands cramping." Counting the money he decides to speak on the murder. "You know, I didn't thank you for having my back that night, I wish you didn't have to but I know you didn't have a choice." Keeping with my count "I know man, the situation presented itself, I just reacted that's all." "You proved yourself to me Karessa', I can trust you with anything. Let me asked you, why didn't you run with the loot?"

I stopped my count and looked him in his eyes "Because it wasn't a reason for me to run. For what, I'm a loyal person, you could have done this job with anyone but you chose me. I take that into consideration, plus I'm doing great for myself so I don't have to do that." "Good attitude to have in this business, I didn't think honor amongst thieves even exist anymore, you proved me wrong. If it's anything you need from me, don't hesitate to ask I got your back Karessa'." After that we felled silent and continue to finish counting. Then I remember I got a bill counter in my living room closet. I haven't used it in a while since I already knew how much I would receive from the other jobs I've been doing. When we finished, the table was the same color of a meadow. Stacks of cash stretched from one end of the table to the next.

Eighty-six thousand dollars was smiling back at us. Forty-three thousand a piece, it gets no better than this. This is just chump change really compared to the real prize waiting in that bag over there.

We had to have a drink after this, a stiff hard drink. I broke out the cognac, marijuana, miniature cigars and clicked on my play list. Since I was in a good mood I wanted to see what Samara was doing. She just made it home but was willing to come over to my place. I began to put up my stash and Fernando began to do the same inside a duffel bag he brought with him. It took Samara about thirty minutes to arrive. I see she has a new tattoo on her left calve and a tennis bracelet. Giving her a hug I introduce her to Fernando. "By the look of things it looks like y'all having some sort of a celebration." she says.

Pouring her a glass I said "Something like that you can say." With a devious smile on her face, she lifts her glass to her lips, held it there than took a small sip. In just that instance the atmosphere changed from sunny to cloudy not quite rainy yet.

I'm trying to read her thoughts, it's like she wants to say something but forcing to keep her tongue in her mouth. The dead air consumed the room, the only thing that could be heard is my music I was playing and I turned the volume down to ten. Swishing the liquor around in his glass Fernando got up and asked to use my bathroom. While he's in my bathroom I had to ask Samara. "Hey is there something wrong?" Speaking assertively to me she says

"Why are you asking me that?"
"Because the way you are looking, sort of grim." "Grim, no it's nothing wrong with me, do you have a problem?" "No I don't, I wanted you to meet my man because since we are all hustlers maybe you two or all of us can do some jobs together." With a wicked smirk "Your man huh, when did that happen?" "What, you know I didn't mean it that way, my friend, my Conrad, my amigo now you stop me at a phrase that you can understand Samara."

By now Fernando enter the living room. "Karessa', sorry I have to cut my visit short, but I got somewhere I needs to be." Staring at Samara with the evil eye, I turned my head to focus on him. "Ok baby, I'm glad you were able to spend some time with me, maybe this Saturday if you're not doing anything we could hook up?" Catching on from what I'm doing from my eye contact to him. "Sure sexy, I will definitely make time for you, I'm mad I have to leave now ma', but I promise I will miss you every minute of the day." I motioned over to him, switching my ass hard enough to crack the pavement. I know Samara is burning up inside, even if she knows I'm just digging in her emotions. "I left my bag by the table, do you mind getting it for me?" "Anything for you daddy, I was hoping you left it so you would have a reason to come back or I could of brought it to your house." "Damn I love that walk of yours Karessa' it turns me the fuck on."

"My walk is just the appetizer, wait until you taste the meal, love will be the only word you could say."

Once I gave him his bag we had a long passionate kiss. It made him drop his bag so he can squeeze my ass and hold me tight. Slightly peeking at Samara, I can see the steam rise from her head. Her eyes squinting I can barely see her pupils. In my mind I'm laughing like I just heard a Bernie Mac joke. When we stopped I made sure she saw me rub my hand across his penis area. Fernando picked up his bag looked at Samara, smiled and said "Nice meeting you Samantha." "The name is Samara asshole" "Sorry didn't mean any harm, when you get to know me you will see I'm not an asshole." She says "Whatever."

After he left out the door I turn around and Samara was snatching her purse off the table. "I'll see you later Karessa.'" as she stormed towards me and the door. "Wait a minute, are you mad?" "No, I just got some things to do, so I got to go." "When I talked to you earlier Samara you just made it home and decided to come over. Now you got an attitude for some reason, I'm sorry but I didn't sleep with you last night." "Karessa' I'm not in the mood for jokes and bullshit, you didn't have to ask me to come over so I can see your little boyfriend." "Samara, Fernando is not my boyfriend where'd you get that shit from I don't know. I invited you over because I thought we could form an alliance, make money together. You came in here assuming, all we were doing is celebrating our robbery we did. If I was on some fucking him would I had called you to come over, does that make any sense?"

Standing there with a dumbfound look. "Ok, why didn't you tell me he was here when you called me?" "Does it matter I didn't tell you he was here, you know what, you can leave." "That's how you feel Karessa'?" "Yes, I need some alone time for myself, I don't need this negative energy soaking up my sunshine, so please just go." Turning the door knob I pulled open and gesture her with my free hand to leave. "Ok, I'll drop your money and the new client's information off to you tomorrow night, I'll call you." "Please do." Slamming the door I smiled because I'm not really angry with her but she did irritate me. I did not expect that reaction from her, she acted like she caught us stealing from her. It's something more to this I'll investigate that later but for now, I got to figure a way to get rid of these diamonds.

CHAPTER 12

I HAVE A FRIEND

The next morning I packed up my laptop, put on one of my cute outfit and headed to the coffee spot. Doing some research on how to move diamonds, to tell you the truth I don't even know where to start. Look who's calling me, policeman Malone, I haven't heard from him in a while. Must have been too busy for me I guess. "Hello." "Hello Ms. Vault, it's been a while." "Excuse me, who is this?" "Aw ok, we going to play this game, its Darius, Darius Malone." "I used to know a Darius Malone, police officer turning detective once, but somehow he felled off the face of the earth."

Laughing "Oh really, maybe he was busy taking that detective test he mention to you about and had to cram for it." "So, did he take the test and if he did what was the result?" He paused for a moment before he answered. "He passed at the top of his class how about that Ms. Vault?"

"Wow, congratulations Darius I'm so proud of you, I knew you would do it." "Thank you Karessa', that means a lot coming from you, what are you doing right now?" "I'm at the coffee spot tapping on my laptop like some yuppie, why do you ask?" "I thought maybe we could get something to eat, just to celebrate me passing my exam." "From test to exam, exam makes it seems like you worked so hard but I like it, sure why not." Sounding excited he says "Ok, where would you like to eat?" "How about we do this Mr. Malone, I want to take you out tonight, you spend nothing, you don't even have to drive, everything is on me would you like that?" "You sure, I don't mind paying." "Don't worry about it big daddy, Ms. Vault is not rich, not yet but I'm doing pretty well for myself, now you just be ready around 8 o' clock, text me your address and I'll handle the rest."

I can feel him smiling over the phone. "Confidence, I like that, it's a date, don't be late." "You just make sure you dress fly, smell good so I can show off some eye candy, good bye Detective Malone." "Later, Ms. Vault." I am really proud of him, I forgot about that exam. I thought maybe he lost interested, it really didn't matter if he had I can't let him get to close anyway. To have an authority figure in your pocket is good though, but to have a crooked one is priceless.

On the way home I got a few things I needed for the night with Darius. Getting ready for the night I hear someone bellowing my name outside. What the hell is going on and who in the hell is that. Feeling somewhat peeved I raised my window and screen up with force. Looking around I hear Karessa', then I looked straight down. It's Dorothy, why is she yelling my name out here as if she's at a ball game. "Dorothy what the hell is wrong with you, why are you

screaming my name in the street?"
"I'm so sorry Karessa' but I wanted
to tell you I'm still waiting on my
check, I wasn't coming upstairs
that's why I was calling your name."
I wish I had an anvil I would drop it
on her head like a cartoon. I put on
my sweet voice "Dorothy could you
come up here please, I need to talk
to you about something." I didn't
even wait for her to knock on the
door, I listened for her footsteps,
when she took that last step I
snatched her inside my apartment.

I threw her up against the wall with
my left forearm in her throat and a
knife beside her left jaw. Her eyes
expanded to the size of tea saucers,
holding her breath I can tell she was
praying in her mind that I don't kill
her. "Bitch let me explain

something to you I'm not one of your buddies on the block, not one of your get high friends. With that being said don't you ever in your life scream, yell, bellow, shout, any adjective with my name included, I will shove this knife so far inside you that you will bleed more than the 28th day of the month, do you feel me coming?" She could have been a mute the way she was scared to speak. "BITCH, DO YOU HEAR ME?" Opening her mouth she meow it out like a kitten. "Yes, I'm so..." Before she could finish I said "SHUT UP! Yes is all I needed, so what's up with my money?" "That's what I was trying to tell you Karessa' my check didn't come yet, it might be here tomorrow or Monday, I just need a little more time?" I release my forearm from her neck. "Ok, next time come to my place and tell me, I don't like my name being projected in the air for the world to hear. I keep to myself and have a small network of people I deal with. I like to help anyone in need but don't take my kindness for weakness." With her head down she says "I promise this will never happen again." "When you get the cash you owe me slide it under my door, don't knock, just slide it and be inconspicuous. Now relieve yourself from my apartment."

This will be the last time I deal with that lunatic, whoever was outside the building now knows my name and not just that, knows where I live. But it's my fault for being good natured, I'm going to have to switch that up. Let me continue to get ready for Mr. Malone. When I was done, I'm going to knock men in their seats damn I look fine if I should say myself as I look in the mirror. Everything red, from my toes to my lips, temptation will be inevitable. These heels helps the booty go pop and the calves look strong not muscular. Chocolate strawberry lip gloss will have him wondering how strong my head game is. Walking to my car some of the wolves out lurking the streets are howling at me, thanks for the compliments fellows that make a girl feel special.

Reaching his house I parked in the drive way and went to ring the doorbell. Opening up his door I was talking about myself but this man here has the physique of a God. His suit is hitting his body perfectly, every angle tightly fitting each muscle that stands out. Is he a detective or an athlete?

"Good evening Karessa', my don't you look gorgeous, I'm mean incredibly stunning." "Thank you Darius, the feeling is mutual I like that cranberry suit and the man in it, you look very luxurious." (Shifting his tie) "I do, don't I." As we laugh I made sure to touch him on his chest just to get a free feel. "So Karessa' what do you have planned for us tonight, I can't wait for the city to see you on my arm." "Then what are we waiting for Mr. Malone your chariot awaits." I took him to a little swanky scenery that I ever seen. It looks like life imitating art it should be hung in a museum somewhere. Telling by Darius face expression he didn't expect this, I might have some hood in me but I am a classy bitch. "This is unexpected you know you didn't have to do all of this Karessa'." "I know I didn't but I wanted to, besides I haven't been out in a long time, it feels good to get dressed up and paint the town red." "Yes, paint the town red that's exactly what you're doing." After we ate we did some dancing and then took a stroll on the boardwalk.

The breeze coming off the ocean is light but just enough to keep us cool since the night is unseasonably warm. Not too many people around, it feels like we're on a private beach. "Karessa', where do you see yourself in five to ten years from now?" Watching the moon glow transfer down to the water "My own business up and running making me uncountable money, in other words rich then wealthy." "I can go for that, have you thought what kind of business that can put you in a racket of being rich then wealthy?" "I want to have my hand in multiple areas like stocks, executive producer of movies, even in the diamond business."

"I thought you dealt in the stock market already?" Damn, forgetting the lie I told him about the profession I was in. "Yes I am, but what I mean is with the big boys you know Nasdaq companies type of stock marketing." "Aw ok, I understand." Whew, I thought my lie was about to fall like a house of cards. "Those are some nice areas to be in, the diamond business, I have a friend that's an appraiser and he makes a hell of a living off of it."

Are the angels shining down on me or this just my lucky day, rather lucky night? "Oh really, that's a profession I would love to know more about, you think I can meet your friend one day?" "Sure, matter of fact this Sunday we going to catch the football game at the sports bar, you're welcome to come." "I will love to, how about we wrap this night up with a night cap at your house." "Luckily I clean up just in case we did go back to my house, no I'm just kidding I keep my house sparkling." Back at his house he poured us a couple of glasses of

Moscato and played some enchanting relaxing music. It felt like a scene from some romantic movie. As we talked the night away we got up from the couch and danced. Before I knew it our lips were locked and my dress hit the floor quicker than popcorn out of a child's hand. It was amazing; I had to cum about ten times if not more. Darius wasn't short on the size either I will definitely be wrestling with that anaconda again.

CHAPTER 13

MEETING MR. LANDON

The next morning when I got home I hopped in the shower with a big smile on my face. I really needed that night get my mind off of Samara and her craziness. Speaking of Samara, she hadn't called me about my money and dropping off the paperwork. Giving her a ring but it went straight to her voicemail. "Hey chick it's me, you didn't call me yesterday, trying to see what's going on with that package call me." I wouldn't be surprised if she's still upset about the other night and really I don't care. Just give me my c-notes and we can leave our friendship at the door. That Sunday I went to meet Darius and his diamond appraisal friend. I arrived thirty minutes after the game started on purpose to make an entrance. Everybody is inside cheering and booing our home town team's achievements and failures.

Darius and his friend is sitting in the second room, this bar is nice, flat screens, video games and all. I'll have to come here some time just to have a drink and mingle. He spotted me about three seconds into entering the room. He wave for me to come to their table. He got up to hug me like he missed me "Hey beautiful." "Hey there yourself handsome, and I guess this is your friend." Scooting his chair back to stand up, he extended his hand out. "Hello Ms. Vault, I'm Demond, Demond Landon." I know it's wrong what I was thinking but this man is so fine. His hand is like a pillow but his grip was so firm that my temperature rose up in my body a couple degrees. That smile is dangerous and his name sounds powerful and that accent. I don't know if Darius notice but I broke the hand shake rule, instead of releasing at three seconds, I took six. "Nice to meet you Demond and please call me Karessa', we don't have to be so formal." "No problem Karessa', I know Darius said you were beautiful but I think that's an understatement, you are absolutely stunning." He is about to make my head pop off, stunning, me, wow I like that. "Well thank you Mr. Landon." "Karessa' you better stop playing, you just asked me not to be formal I expect the same." "Ok, Demond I can do that."

"Now that you two met, Karessa' wants to learn about the appraiser profession, isn't that right Karessa'?" My mind didn't compute the information it just received from Darius. I'm still stuck on Demond but then it finally processed about ten seconds later. "Um yea right, Darius tells me you make a pretty good living being a diamond appraiser and I am considering moving in that direction." "Yes this is a very good field to get in but I'm a jewelry appraiser and much more, I do it all, it takes some studying but it's not impossible. The best way to become a successful one is to become an intern and since I'm an independent jewelry appraiser you can learn from the best. So, how about it Karessa', are you willing to learn?"

Without a hesitation in my responds "Yes, we can I start?" "If you want you can start tomorrow, that will be excellent, 9am, just be prepared to be there for most of the day ok?" "Cool, I will be there." Reaches inside his jacket pocket and pulls out his business card. "Here's my card, it has the address to my place don't be late, lateness means it's not important to you." "Don't worry about me, I'll be there I'm an early bird anyway." "Now that y'all finished having y'all little meeting, can we enjoy the game please, we are getting our ass kicked. We need more hot wings and a pitcher of beer." You can enjoy the game I'm going to enjoy the company. See there I go again, I'm going to keep it professional no need to cause any drama plus I need to figure out how to get him to appraise these diamonds without arousing suspicion.

CHAPTER 14

BLIND SIDED

After the game I spent some time with Darius at his house. We watched a movie and just relax and converse. I got up around 6:30am the next morning to get ready, made a stop to get me some breakfast before making it to Demond's shop. Approaching his shop I got a little nervous but I pushed on. Pushing the buzzer for entry I glance down the street then he buzz me in to enter. "Good morning, Demond." "Ah yes, good morning, Karessa' I see you made it." "Yes I told you I will come, I made sure to get me some sleep and I had breakfast, now I'm all yours." "Good, well today

I'm going to show you different names and shapes of diamonds. I have a book for you, I want you to just chill and read for a couple of hours while I handle some work. Once I'm done then I will go over the book with you." "Sounds like a plan."

I sat in the back, cracked open the book and began to read. A couple of hours later I hear someone come through the shop front door. I took a peek around the corner, its two guys talking to Demond. Not trying to judge but they look kind of shady, I mean they have on some expensive suits but look like they work for the underworld. I know, too many gangster movies but these two fit the part to a T. I rushed back in the room because Demond came walking towards my way. He's knocking on the door as he's opening it. "Hey Karessa', I need to make a quick run, I'm going to lock the front and put my I'll be back sign on it. If you need to step out for anything take this key and go in and out the back door to the alley." "Ok, how long will you be if you don't mind me asking?" "About an hour no longer than two, once I get back we will talk."

Oh this man got a smile that can light up a stadium and those pearly whites in his mouth, just freshness. "I'll be ready Demond, see you later." I stood half way around the corner and watched them get inside a luxury car. This got to be the life and I want to be a part of it.

I walk around the store, being curious seeing if I can find anything I shouldn't be seeing. When I went to the back, it's a big steel door with an electric combination lock on it that's towering over me. I know what's inside of there but I'm wondering how much is inside of there or how much it's worth. I went back to read and began to dozed off but I was awaken by the alarm system. It's Demond entering the shop, so I grab my book and pretended I was reading.

"Hello Karessa', were you ok while I was gone?" "Yes, just sitting here reading like you asked me to do." "All you did was read, you didn't do anything else, didn't go anywhere?" "Umm, no just stayed in this room and read." Then he shows me his phone, it was footage of me walking around his shop, even me sleeping before he came in. "Obvious you didn't know I have cameras all around but it is a jewelry shop Karessa'." Surprised "Look I'm so sorry Demond, I didn't mean any harm, just being curious that's all." "It's ok Karessa' I expected you would snoop, I would have done it myself. Let me show you something." He took me to a room that is locked. Once we walked inside and he clicked the light switch on it looked like he brought me to a diamond emporium. Each side of the room sparkled, each diamond taking turns to shine. "You know what Karessa', it's something about you. I know I just met you yesterday but my gut is telling me you are no average woman. I can tell you're very intelligent, highly skilled in some areas, am I right?"

I'm trying to read where he is coming from with this and how he can tell much about me from a brief conversation that I revealed nothing about me. "I guess you can say that, I don't mind getting my hands dirty if I have to." Shaking and pointing his finger at me "Getting your hands dirty if you have to, now see, I like that answer that means to me to achieve your objective it's nothing you wouldn't do. Answer me this, have you ever killed anyone, man, woman or an alien?" Puzzled about why he asked me this "No I haven't, but won't hesitate if I have to." "See now, my spider man senses are tingling and it's telling me you have.

And not just have but recently like a couple of Fridays ago, I can still smell the gun power off your hand." With those words falling out his mouth the inside of my body broke into freeze mode, my tongue felt like a desert, heart pumping something fierce. "What are you talking about Demond, where are you getting this from?"

"Listen Karessa', let me tell you a little something about myself, I don't play games I am one of the most dangerous individuals you will meet in your life. Fernando, ah the handsome Fernando, the guy you did the bank job with is dead I cancelled him after he left your apartment. (Picking up different diamonds and holding them to the light) He came out your building

right into his coffin. He is actually
the one who brought my attention
to you, it just took a few taps on the
computer from my computer wizard
to find you but it was by chance that
day he happens to see you, the plan
was for him to run into you in front
of your building. All he had to do
was bring me the diamonds, only
one fucking job and how did he
repay me. By plotting to vacate the
city with my merchandise, the
money was his and whoever he
wanted to share it with I didn't care.
(Becoming angry) Just bring me the
fucking stones, by the way how
much did you make from that
heist?"

Speaking softly I said "Forty-
three." "Forty-three thousand
dollars?" he asked. "Yes, a piece

and he split the diamonds with me, look I didn't know." Walking closer to me "I know you didn't Karessa', you were a pawn better yet a casualty in his plan, not our original plan. Greed will always spoil the mission it taints the very existence of the moral and fiber that the criminal establishment is built on. After I saw your resume and all the things he said he taught you plus your ambition, I had to admit I was impressed, especially your being a woman. See the female species always have something to prove to her male counterpart, you know like she can do the job which I love. You are perfect Ms. Vault, sorry you did say let's not be so formal, Karessa' for my future endeavors. I'm assuming you still have my

precious in your possession, right?"
"Yes it is and I just want to make this right."

"You will, you will Karessa' because now (Grabbing my face and releasing it) you work for me and me only. Let me ask you this, how did Fernando explain the way he got out of jail?" Inhaling then exhaling "He said since he gave me his gun and mask the police had nothing on him, they held him for forty-eight hours then released him and charged him with evading the police." Laughing he says "Well that is the story we told him to say and at least he did that right, but actually your friend Officer Malone better known as Darius just turned detective (pausing) just to let you know, he's been a detective for about seven years or more now. He's also on my payroll; he didn't knock on your door that day and strike up a conversation with you by mere coincidence. That was just to make sure we had the right Karessa' Vault and yes we have the right one, you are very beautiful Karessa' and you're built perfect for your new line of work."

Still semi oblivious to the whole situation "May I ask, what will this be, I mean the work you are talking about?" "Yes you may, this line of work or career whatever is the type of work you been doing all along, professional thief, just on a higher scale. You told Detective Darius Malone you want unaccountable money, well welcome to the world of unaccountable money." As he rose his hands in the air like a preacher, with a slow turn introducing me to his dimension of criminology. My mind went dead, actually stuck on how did I fall for this. This is the perfect example of all money is not good money. Something simple as a bank robbery landed me in a life I didn't ask for, not ask for but forced into. I got to figure a way out of this mess but for now I know I must play his game, his twisted game.

Maybe Samara had a vibe about Fernando to make her react the way she did. I'm usually a good judge of people but I was blinded by the fact we serviced in the Marines together. And he's the one who taught me and help me elevate my skills to become a more sophisticated criminal. Still, why me, this not making no sense. "Karessa' this is what I want you to do, take this paper, meet me here tomorrow morning, erase this place from your memory bank. I will give you instructions from there, understand?" "I understand." I started to walk towards the door then he says "Don't forget my diamonds and don't try to run, I have eyes everywhere, I know you love your parents, it would be a shame if they come up missing." Stopping me in my tracks from the statement he made "I will have it Demond, no worries."

I didn't drive straight home, I called my mother and let her know I was coming by their house. Fearing for their life more than my own I just wanted to check on them, spend some time with them. Trying to keep my mind off of Demond I took them out for a bite to eat, looking around as we sat for any suspicious faces hiding within the crowd.

Feeling the sting from the pressure of this situation with my so called new boss, I will have to think of a plan to escape, save me and my love ones. It's hard trying to smile when you have a problem weighing heavy on your head. But I keep my composure and made sure my parents enjoyed their time with me. I know the life I chose is a deadly one but I never dreamed of it pulling the two people I hold dear to my heart in the middle of it. Not wanting to leave my mother and father yet we went to the local mall, did a little shopping, I even took them to catch a matinee. After some ice cream I dropped them off at home but I went inside their residence with them just to satisfy my own nerves. Now heading to my destination I'm preparing myself for the inevitable.

CHAPTER 15

THE RED ROOM

This the first time in a long time I couldn't get any sleep, up until about 3am. Going to the address he gave me it's in a building that's set off by itself with a store front. Two stories high, kind of reminded me of those old gangster hide outs that Capone and his gang would hold illegal beer barrels in. I rang the doorbell three times with two quick knocks like the piece of paper he gave me told me to. When the door opened this huge body guard for the stars looking ass man is on the other side of it. Staring me down as if I rang the wrong bell, he then stepped to the side and gesture to me to enter the premises.

Walking inside he tells me to continue forward to the end of the hallway. I noticed that the store front is really a front, where the store supposed to be it's a bar, a glossy wooden floor, a replica of a 1950 jukebox or maybe it's an original with a table and four chairs pushed under it. Also a large picture of Idi Amin standing with some goons, a glass shelf with mirrors with lights full with multiple liquor bottles. I made it to the end of the hallway where it's another door. Knocking on this door I was told to come in, upon going in Demond is sitting behind this bronze and black shiny desk reflecting whatever is facing it, looking like a mob boss with two henchmen on each side of him. It's another one laying in the cut and one more behind the door.

Demond is leaning back in a plush leather chair that about the size of a King's throne, the window behind him has two long silk curtains with ropes wrapped around them giving the sun some leeway inside. Walls covered with African style paintings and the rug makes me feel like I'm walking on soft fresh grass. The way this place looks on the exterior I would had never expected the interior to be so extravagant. And I haven't been upstairs yet, if I get a chance to make it up there.

"Please sit down Ms. Vault, I'm glad you came. I believe you have something for me." Putting the bag on the desk he let it sit for a second before he reach and picked it up. Pouring it on his desk he smiles as the bag finish dispensing the jewels. He takes out a loupe from inside his suit jacket and holds one of the diamonds in his hand. "Aw yes" he says while slowly twirling the precious with his fingers. After checking out the another one he hands them to one of his soldiers to put up, grab a small trash can from where he is sitting and swept the rest of diamonds with his hand into it.

"Those are glass, just used to fill the bag up. Thank you for bringing me my merchandise, now let's get to business. Look at this photo, the man on it is a Russian jeweler name Andrei Volkov, one of the best, his jewel collection is heaven. He has an event coming up in Las Vegas, it will be wall to wall security but Fernando techniques he taught you will come in handy here, what you learned doing you stint in the Marines and on these mean streets. It will be very useful for the jobs I have lined up for you. (I'm staring at the picture while he's talking.) I have a package for you." One of his goons hands me a yellow envelope. "Inside you will find all the information you need for you to infiltrate and get this rare jewel. You have until Friday morning to learn what's inside that package by that afternoon you should be at the airport preparing to leave for Sin City; this operation must go smooth Karessa'. Try not to leave any bodies either but if you have to be precise with your kill and don't leave a trail that can lead back to you. You must leave now I have another appointment I need to tend to."

While I'm getting up out of my chair so I could exit his phone rings. Before I could turn the knob on the door Demond says "Karessa' wait, I will like you to accompany me upstairs in my red room I have something to show you." My feet turned cold, felt like I'm stuck in harden cement. Swallowing the hunk of saliva that produced in my mouth he came walking pass me with his shirt open and flapping in the air then I follow suit behind him. His two henchmen are trailing behind us as we enter an elevator and went up to the second floor.

When the doors separated Demond pushed up a switch that made a sound like it shifting gears for train tracks but it turned the lights on.

It was one large floor with half of it filled with containers. Containers of what I don't know. It had a bit of a stench, some foul aroma that was weak but strong enough to make me cover my nose. The windows are painted black so no sunlight can come inside, its plastic covering the entire floor. The walls are painted blood red, moving towards the other end I can see a table with some device connected to it. Once we get closer I can see a buzz saw and the table is actually a conveyor belt with a few empty containers around it. Stains on the blade and the steel part of the conveyor belt can be visibly seen.

Demond tells one of his henchmen to tell the other to bring him in. He goes through this steel door that he had to pull to the side, its moving turtle like because of the weight and size of it. When he comes back out its three other men following him, two big guys like the one at the door earlier in all black with black leather aprons on. But the third one had on a blindfold, hands tied behind his back and stripped naked. Demond reaches behind one of the containers and brings up an axe and this shoe box size stone block. Slapping the axe handle in his hand he's motioning in the direction of the victim I guess

I should call him because that's how he looks.

"Break his ass down to his knees and show him no mercy" he told the guys in the aprons. One of his goons punches him in his stomach, the other one smashed him in the back of his head that's when he dropped to his knees coughing and spiting. Demond turns to me "Karessa' I want you to watch and learn. When you steal or take from me that is a show of disrespect." As he making his speech one henchmen is putting the stone under their victim's neck. "When I give you work believe me, you will make plenty of money from it. So if you find yourself wanting to betray me by lying to me when I caught you with your filthy hands inside my pockets, I rather for you to just spit in my face."

Putting the axe over shoulder and standing three feet away on the side of the man who neck is on the stone, without a blink of the eye he swung the axe downward onto his neck. The contact of the axe cutting through the flesh and bone of his neck sounded gruesome. His head felled to the floor, his body was still gyrating from the shock but Demond just zoned out, swinging the axe slicing through the corpse with pure anger. I turned my head and closed my eyes. He stopped and turned towards me with blood pieces of flesh splatter on his clothes face and hands he says "You better keep your eyes on me bitch."

Without a second thought I put my undivided attention back on him. He kept swinging until it was no more large parts for him to chop. Tossing the axe he told them to clean this shit up and told me to come as he put his arm around me as he forcibly guides me back to the elevator. From behind I heard them start the conveyor belt and buzz saw. By his grip on me I can tell his intense anger is strengthening him because he's still boiling from the massacre I just witnessed.

"Do you understand what the process is now Karessa', that's right chop him up to pieces, make him disappear like he never exist. The lesson here is this (Whispering) keep your hands where they belong and you want end up in my red room better yet my death room."

Once we reached the elevator and the doors opened up he rode down with me. When we got to the front door he pointed his blood soak index finger in my face and says to me "Do not end up upstairs in my building Karessa'. If I have to meet you there you should know the outcome will either give you horns or a halo, depending if God wants you or if Lucifer blocks your passage, now you're dismissed." On the other side of the door I staggered around the corner and regurgitated, some splashing on my shoes and the bottom of my pants. Now I know what the stench is, it's the stench of death. Walking somewhat off balance to my car I got in and put my head on the steering wheel. Looking back up the only thing I could see is that axe and the grim reaper expression on Demond's face. The sound of it slicing through that man flesh, bones cracking like tree branches. My stomach's empty but I don't want anything to eat, I don't think I can hold any food down at this moment.

CHAPTER 16

THE REASON I CAME

Back at my home base I just got ripped. For the next few days the only thing I was doing was getting drunk getting high as I can possibly get and studying the contents of the package. I was in my own shell it wasn't anything that could get me out of it. By the time Friday arrived I knew what I needed to know inside out, feeling like I just crammed for a secret agent examination. My phone started ringing, on the caller ID it showed Samara name. Upon answering it I told her we will have to talk when I get back I'm on my way to Las Vegas for the weekend. She wanted to go but I had to decline her offer because of the nature of my trip.

Touching down in Vegas I took a cab to the hotel where I will be staying. Using the fake ID with the alias I was provided with to get my key card for my room. Sitting my bag on my bed the room phone started ringing. When I picked it up the voice at the other end with a heavy African accent says "Welcome to Las Vegas Ms. Vault, I will need you to meet me in the hotel restaurant I won't be hard to find just use your nose and follow the cigar scent." Then he hung up, I threw some water on my face and took a swig of mouthwash to goggle.

Going through the lobby area posters of the jewelry event by

Andrei Volkov is displayed. Entering the restaurant I glance around, walking down the three steps. I can see smoke floating in the air in the distance, the scent of a cigar is burning but the person that smoking it has his back to the entrance. It must be the one who called me I'm thinking as I am headed towards the cigar smoke.

Have a seat the person says when I was about two feet behind him. Seating down he ask me how was my flight and I answered pretty cool. From there he offered me to order something but I declined, then he got straight to business. "My name is Allabesi but you call me Alla, did you study the package that was given to you?" "Yes I did but I didn't know I would be having an escort as well." "Even though you are assuming it, it's true. But first I'm going to have a car pick you up when you leave here you will be taken to our tailor to have a special dress made for the event. The dress will be made with two compartments, one for the jewel the other one for your gun. Also a flash bomb and other gadgets you can use if you are in danger plus a gun holder for a two shooter you can strap around your upper thigh.

It's going to be basically simple Karessa', it will be two security officers guarding the room where the diamond will be, it's also a combination lock on the door to the room, this device will scramble the lock to find the combination so you can get inside. Once you're in, retrieve the diamond off the pillow replacing it with a fake diamond, remove it slowly and replace it slowly so you want trigger off the alarm. You will only have three minutes to complete and exit right it'll be a door at the end of the hall. Leaving out of it, it will be a car in the alley with the doors unlocked and keys already in the ignition. In the **GPS** put in the address I give you and that will be your destination, it will be a change of clothes there, once you change clothes I will take you to the airport and head home wait for instruction from there understand?"

"Yes but I have one question, what about the other information I had to learn about, when will I use that?" Laughing before he spoke "Never, the boss uses that just to see how much your brain can store in a small amount of time and I can tell you're a bright woman Karessa' because you learned it. Look I know Demond have you over a crocodile pit, this is what he do to people he has something on but it's always a way to get out." Sitting here listening to him, wondering why is he telling me this. Maybe he's trapped also trying to figure his own way out or just trying to see my reaction and notify Demond of what I said. He only can know about me from what he was told by Demond or whoever feeds him the information. "A way out huh, how you propose I go about finding a way out?" "Well the only antidote is studying your enemy and learning your enemy is the best way to get rid of your enemy." "I'll keep that in mind but now I just want to complete this mission." "I understand, take this case with you, it has a gun and a silencer inside, when the time comes use it. Come, I will walk you out and I will be to pick you up at eight, be ready."

Walking me out, he took his phone out and sent out a text. Stepping on to the street a black four door Cadillac truck pulls up in front of the hotel. Allabesi opens up the back passenger side door for me to sit down. "After you visit the tailor he will take you anywhere you want to go, this is your transportation until tomorrow evening. See you tomorrow night Karessa.'" he then closed the door.

Once I was done with getting fitted for my dress I went casino hopping, releasing the stress and pressures of the mission. Having a few drinks, treating myself to dinner, 2 o' clock in the morning is when I made it back to my room and crashed.

That night, Allabesi came to my room he was in a tuxedo looking pretty astonishing I should say. "Wow Karessa' you look fabulous if you don't mind me saying so." "Thank you Alla, you clean up pretty nice yourself." "Thank you, are you ready Ms. Vault." As he extended his arm out towards me I wrapped mines around his and we left out the door. Riding over to the event we went over the plan one more time. Once inside we walk around checking out the displays of diamonds reading the description of the rocks. Allabesi is pretending to discuss about the jewelry but actually showing me where they keeping the precious I have to take, scoped out the security detail and alternative exits. By this time the room engulfed in a clapping sound, when we turned around the host of the event Andrei Volkovo comes out. Laced in all white with body guards on each side he commenced to wave his hands as to stop the attendees clapping. Within three minutes into his speech Allabesi checked his phone then whispered in my ear.

I went into the washroom checking all the stalls then step inside one of the stalls, took my weapon out of the compartment on my dress and put the silencer on the gun. Knowing the witch hour was approaching I put the gun in my purse. Leaving back out to floor of the event Andrei Volkovo was still in the mist of his speech. Then I heard a commotion ensuing out in the hall way area, three of the security officers on the floor of the event exited to the ruckus. Knowing that was my gun shot to start the race but before I could motion to the back where the diamond is at I had to take care of the one security officer blocking the entrance. Even though he's standing there he's paying more attention to the noise seeping through the event doors.

I came up behind him in one full motion I snapped his neck and dragged him out of view.

Proceeding towards the two security officers guarding the diamond, "What are you doing back here Miss?" one of them says. "Sorry, I thought this way lead to an exit." I replied. "No it doesn't, I suggest you go back the way you just came lady." I reach inside my purse "Ok I just need to show you something on my phone real fast." The steel came out and I pointed the gun at them in 3D. Two clean head shots BANG! BANG!, both bodies fell, I walked to the vault and connected the decoder on the key pad.

Come on I said as the decoder switching to different combinations trying to find pay dirt. I'm anxious, hand shaking while I'm holding the knob to the door. One beep the screen blinking access, I turned the knob and pull. The door is ajar and I can tell from the smell its money in here. Pulling it fully it felt like I'm about to enter King Tut's tomb. There it is, face to face with the reason I am in Las Vegas, it's no turning back now. Easing the stone from its perch, I lifted it with the grace of a snail. Before I could replace it with the fake diamond I was startled by a noise and dropped the diamond back on the cushion.

The security alarm was triggered and I snatched the diamond and ran to the exit Allabesi told me to go to where the car will be waiting for me outside. Once I reached it, I pushed the release bar to go out. But it's locked, panicking but trying to keep my cool the stilettos that I got from the tailor the heels and top of the sole are built to disconnect from the bottom so I can maneuver better like I'm wearing sneakers.

I retreated back in the other direction where I came from. One of the other security officers happened to be coming in the opposite way. She looked down at the two guards on the floor, then back up at me. Before she could take her gun out the holster I let off two shots, hitting her in the arm and neck. While her soul is choosing life or death I went pass her and across the event room floor. Making it to the end of the hall confused on which way to go until the bullets that came whizzing around me help me choose one expeditiously.

Reaching a door half way in the direction I'm running, when I entered inside it was a stairway. I hit the stairs upward, skipping up some in the process. Come back here a voice echoed through the stair well, by the sound the individual's temperamental. Guns blasting at me, I aimed downward returning fire. I can hear one on his walkie talkie giving my location but once I reached the top I busted through the door leading to the roof.

Sprinting but not knowing what I'm going to do next I slammed on the breaks when I got to the other side of the roof. Turning around the two officers that's chasing me finally made it on the roof. "Put your fucking hands up!" one of them bellowed at me. Looking over the

side of the wall I noticed a parking
garage to the east across the alley.
Moving in closure to me, I laid my
gun down and raised my hands.
After they took a few more steps I
took off running as fast as I can. All
I'm thinking is I saw them do this in
the movies, I know it's crazy but
what other choice I have. Before I
knew it I'm jumping over the wall
and into the night's air, closing my
eyes I landed on the pavement.
Rolling uncontrollably I stopped
when I crashed into the back of a
car's bumper. Laying there for a few
seconds or more, out of breath,
terrified but pleased by the
outcome.

Pulling myself to my feet I limped
my way to the elevator, got off on
the second floor so I could look

onto the street and see if any security officers or police were in vicinity. Not seeing any I saw a taxi parked ten feet away so I ran and hopped in the back seat. Laying low so I wouldn't be seen I gave him the address that Allabesi supplied me with, ducked down in the back seat but not too low so he wouldn't think something is wrong. He drove the way the event is at, my heart beating like I'm staring down the barrel of a gun. Police lights, yellow tape, ambulances, a large crowd with police officers controlling the traffic having any vehicles coming down this street detour.

Once we made it to my destination I had the taxi driver to wait while I went inside. I twist the knob and wondering to myself why the door is unlocked already once inside Allabesi is sitting at a fold out table smoking a cigarette. "I see that you made it here." he says. Leaning back against the door rubbing my knee I said "I need some money to pay the taxi driver." "The taxi driver what do you mean?" "Just pay the driver than I will tell you what happen to me." As he went out I sat down tired and worn out. Coming back in a little winded rushing to pay the driver so he could hear what I had to say. "Tell me now." Allabesi says to me. Telling him how everything went down he's sitting in amazement like he's in the presence of his favorite super hero and enjoying each sentence that falls out my mouth. "You, you are a super woman Karessa', this sounds like something out of an action movie." "You think, why was the fucking door locked, I couldn't get to the car!" Shrugging his shoulders "Karessa' I don't know, one of the guys did the walk through, I don't know if he tested to see if it opened or maybe the people working the event locked it for security measures." "That was pretty fucked up, besides killing the officers guarding the diamond, I had to shot another one also. (Exhaling) You know what let me get dressed so I can catch this flight back home."

Changing clothes I can hear Allabesi talking on his phone in the other room. Couldn't make out much but I did hear him say she has the package and it's about to be airborne. Ok, ok we are about to head towards the airport right now.

"Who were you talking to?" I asked. "Who else, the boss man, I had to call him once you made it here. He's keeping a human GPS on the diamond; I have to call him once we're heading to the airport." "I bet he does, what a trust worthy man, he's the hit at every party." Laughing at what I just said "Right, a real comedian, let's go so you can catch your flight." Riding to the airport all I'm thinking about is my bed and days of sleep. My knees are swollen, I scraped my forearm and I have a massive headache. Walking me to the terminal Allabesi and I exchanged good byes. "Maybe I'll see you again Karessa', hopefully under different circumstances."

"Only the future holds that truth, later Alla."

Boarding the plane I couldn't wait to sit down and sleep for the next five hours. Being awoken by a few taps on the shoulder, the stewardess told me we are about to land. Coming out the terminal, I went to the parking garage to get my car just walking through it I'm having flashbacks of Las Vegas. Getting inside my car I leaned back in the seat and let out a sigh of relief just glad to be back in my city. Making it home I ran me a hot bath, fill the tub with so many bubbles they're spilling onto the floor, put on some meditating music and rolled up some weed. If I have ever wanted to be home this is definitely the time. The heat from the water is attentive to my bones that are aching. I never thought in a thousand years I would be in the position that I am in. The hour in the tub did my body some justice, I rub myself down with alcohol and it felt so soothing. It was lights out before I knew it.

CHAPTER 17

IT GETS DEEPER

When I finally open my eyes again it was twelve o' clock on the head. Vision blurry and trying to get my focus straight I could hear my phone beep. Listening for where the beeping sound is coming from I notice it on the opposite side of the bed. I rolled over even though my body felt stiff and picked it up off the floor, dammit I missed ten calls from Demond. Calling him back he answered "Where the hell are you?" "I'm sleep sorry, the action from Vegas worn me out." I said. "I don't want to hear your fucking excuses you get to my office pronto." As I was about to say ok he hung the phone up.

Body is hurting but I force myself to get dress and popped a couple of pain pills. I can't wait for those to kick in. When I get to my door it was an envelope laid on the floor that somebody pushed under it. Ripped it open it was a hundred dollar bill, Dorothy's money she owes me. I guess me snatching her off her feet really sink into that fat head of hers. Really I got this other shit on my mind, this Demond shit, if she didn't pay it back I wouldn't haven't thought about it.

On my way to meet Demond I see an old acquaintance of mines. Low and behold, Cody going into the corner liquor store. I guess I can take a few minutes out of my busy schedule to see what's been going on with him. I parked my car and put my gun on my lap and waited. Five minutes goes pass and he's walking out with a brown paper bag, looks like he brought himself a beer. Jumping out on him as he going pass my car I slammed the car door that made him jerk and turn around.

"What's up Cody, you know you're a hard man to find in these streets nowadays." Eyes wide open looking like he's staring at the end of his time on earth but of course he is. Nervously he says "Hey Karessa' how you been girl, I've been looking for you, everybody said you been chilling in the hood on and off."
"Have you Cody, because far as I

can remember you left me hanging at the house that we both supposed to cash out on, that's what I remember." "Look Karessa' I didn't mean for that to happen man, I want to apologize for what I did I didn't mean to stab you in the back." "Not only my back, my front, my sides every side of my soul Cody, we come from the bottom man, we better than this man at least I thought we were." "We are and I can make this right, let me fix..." Before he could finish I said "No way buddy, you only get to burn me once, after that it's infamy. Now come on you know the pecking order, walk in this alley with me so we can finish this conversation." "Karessa' you know these drugs got me right, (Aggressively) look at me I

need help it's so hard out here!"
Not responding to none of the sob
story he's putting out. I knew he
wasn't going to go in the alley with
me willingly, his face expression
showed it.

Because he knew two of us walking
in but only one is coming out. The
only option he has now is to pick
door number two that is to run for
his life and that is what he chose to
do. So I shot him four times hitting
one in his back and one in each leg,
the fourth one missed but he's not
dead, well not yet. Crawling with his
hands that's pulling the weight of his
lower body that's not able to move
because of the bullets I put in him. I
inched up on him, aim my gun to
the back of his head and squeezed.

His soul levitated out of his body into the atmosphere.

Back in my car I sped off down the street adrenaline rushing throughout my veins. I'm not scared either because I'm realizing how easy it is for me to pull the trigger. Killing that security guard at the bank, it was hard for my eyes to stay shut so I could enter dream land. But now I don't even have a second thought, my heart is surrounded by the same ice as an assassin. I don't know if that's a good thing or if I'm becoming one of the heartless and faceless people in this world. But I am noticing the change and with this change, I'm becoming more menacing.

Reaching Demond's place, I go to the door and do the secretive knock and bell ring. Going down the hall to his office I'm contemplating what's he's going to do or say and really, I does not give a fuck. Knocking on his door he says enter. The scene looks like the last time I was here everyone in their same position like it's a portrait. He told me to have a seat but I told him I prefer to stand. Tilting his head to the side and his finger on his lips "Where is my package Karessa'?" I reached inside my jacket pocket pulled out my fist then open it with the diamond sitting in the palm of my hand. Stepping up and extending my hand to him, he took the stone then I stepped back from his desk. "Beautiful, just so damn beautiful, you did well Karessa'. I heard about the door incident and what you had to do after you were jammed up. But you improvise and made the best out of a terrible situation that had your life on the line." "I did what I had to do a true soldier doesn't give up until death plays its card." With a promising look on his face he sees I'm worth more than he even expected.

"You know Karessa' what you did for me and how you handled yourself I have, how can I say it, this secluded club of mercenaries known to the underworld as the Darken Clips and I have an opening." Standing up, turning to the window behind him with his hands clutch behind his back "I want get too much into the details of what they do, but let's just say if you would have decided to vanish with my precious, they have a way of making you reappear again then disappear again, understand." Doing a 180 degree turn from the window Demond walks to where I am standing staring me in my eyes. "Staring in your eyes I can see the coldness, the troubles, the love but the evil you can produce, evilness is good in a bad way. I believe we will have a long relationship, that's what my gut says, but if you prove that to be wrong Ms. Karessa' Vault, I will personally take the most dull knife I have in my collection and force it through your chest to penetrate your cold heart, making sure you have a slow and painful death." I can tell he meant every word he said. Each dark sentence he spoke sent shivers through my body but not enough to put fear in my heart of him. Standing in front of me for a minute after his speech he walks over to his desk, reach inside the top drawer and takes out a white envelope. "This is for you, excellent work, go enjoy yourself I will be in touch." Handing me the envelope, as I reach for it he snatches it back, then with an ominous smile on his face he gives it to me.

Upon leaving the room I can feel his eyes burning through the back of my skull from all of this I don't know if he trust me or not but I know I don't trust him especially that bastard Detective Malone. Mad at myself for fucking him, but that's just more motivation to get him as well as Demond.

Driving, I get to talking to myself, what I did to Cody crossed my mind; all he had to do was be right. His death doesn't bother me because it's justified in my eyes but how do you grow up close with people but they change on you. That's the part that bothers me, but he knows the rules of the streets. I knew one day I would see him again that's why I stopped looking for him. Not even smart enough to take whatever money he got from the job and disappear. I would had in that situation but this one I'm in now I know the only way for me to get out is death and I don't mean mines.

I parked in front of my building about to call Samara when two darken trucks with tinted windows tires screeching blocked me in. The front doors and the back doors of the two trucks flies open, eight men in suits with guns drawn are pointing directly at me. Yelling put your hands up now at me. One of them seized my door handle, opened the door with one hand, snatched me and forced me on the ground. Hand cuff my hands behind my back and put a bag over my head then two of them lifted me up. They proceeded to shove me in one of their trucks with two of them sitting on each side of me. They pulled off faster than when they pulled up on me.

"What did I do?" is what I asked but my question is met with silence, turning corners like they own the streets and no pedestrians should be on them. "So nobody is going to say anything?" I asked, once again not a word or a mumble.

About twenty minutes has passed and I can tell we are going down a garage ramp. I hear a beeping sound then the sound of a garage door opening up. Parking their trucks they snatch me out and rushed me to the elevator like I'm late for a meeting. Snatching the cover off my head they're walking me down a floor that has poor lighting with only one door that's at the other end from where we are walking. Inside the room two of them slams me in the chair, took the cuff off one wrist then locked it to a round steel ring piece made into the table, left out and closed the door.

I'm in complete darkness, silence, fearing the unknown and prepared myself for the worst. I can hear one set of footsteps fainted but echoing down the hall with my heart pounding I'm watching the area of darkness where they brought me in here. Once the footsteps ended the door comes ajar and a hand reaches in flicks the light switch. One light comes on and it's hanging over the table, the scene is mimicking an old detective movie from the 1930's. As the door open further the shadow of the individual is cast on the floor, when it's fully open the shadow appeared on the wall. Then when this individual's face is exposed to me I couldn't believe it, my mouth

just dropped. "Hello Ms. Karessa'
Vault."

THE WORLD OF KARESSA' VAULT

Karessa' Vault is not your average woman. Her life style is a dangerous one. And when you are living this type of life you invite without asking other elements that can be poisonous. Sometimes it's a way to avoid this but when she gets involved with a friend that puts her in a position where she has no choice but to comply. Now trapped in a world that's parallel to her own the only difference is she's not her own boss any more. That's where the plot thickens and she must play the menacing game of Demond Landon. His mind state is heartless and his veins rotate ice inside them. To get from under his thumb will be a task in its own. So the question

becomes not how to get out, but
when to.

- J. Wrice Sr.

I love to thank all the readers that giving my talent a chance. I really appreciate you all. You are the reason I'm glad I am blessed with an imagination that extends the universe. Once again thank you.

About the Author

J. Wrice Sr. is an influential writer and blogger. Coming from the impoverished streets of Chicago South Side, he became to be one of people to help shape the Chicago hip hop community. Being one of the four horsemen who helped started the organization the Ill-State Assassins a crew full of emcees and Dj's that made a huge contribution to the urban music movement in the 80's and 90's Chicago golden era.

The music group he was in Tha Chamba was nominated for a Grammy. Also being a tree that had many roots his organization helped kick start some of Chicago's break out music groups. Now becoming an author, the same way he had ways of writing lyrics that intrigued the mind his book writings are doing the same. He has a way of making you think and open your mind to a whole new world that the imagination will love to explore.

To keep up with the latest news and blogs on

J. Wrice Sr.

www.jwricesr.com